Pesky People are praising Life Is a Movie Starring You...

"This book is not only powerful, but fun and truly inspiring. All of its references are so true to my nostalgic heart—I would have given anything for this book growing up. Jennifur teaches us that being Pesky means loving the cards that we are dealt, and appreciating each day that we have as an opportunity to be smarter and sillier than the day before. Her book blows my mind!"

—Actress Drew Barrymore

"Jennifur is a glam girl after my own heart. I've long been a Pesky Meddling Girl, and with this book you can learn just how to become one of these fabulous creatures. Entertaining and inspiring, this book is the perfect accessory for any wardrobe!"

—Fashion designer Anna Sui

"Why have just fifteen minutes of fame when you can be a star for life! Jennifur Brandt takes us on a glittery, glam, Technicolor ride to Peskyville, giving girls a chance to discover their own inner and outer fabulousness."

—Hillary Carlip, author of *Girl Power*

Life Is a Movie Starring You

The Pesky Meddling Girls™ Guide to Living Your Dreams

By Jennifur Brandt

WARNER BOOKS

A Time Warner Company

WARNER BOOKS, INC., 1271 AVENUE OF THE AMERICAS, NEW YORK, NY 10020

Visit our Web site at www.twbookmark.com

A Time Warner Company

Printed in the United States of America

First Printing: December 2000

10 9 8 7 6 5 4 3 2

Book designed by Jennifur Brandt

*Star on the Cover: Jennifur Brandt
Superstar photographess: Lizzie Brandt
Coiffure creation: Douglas Little
Dreamy gown: Vintage from Jennifur's own archive
Lovely location: Grauman's Chinese Theatre, Hollywood
Inspiration: Marilyn Monroe, Jacqueline Susann and Brigitte Bardot.

Library of Congress Cataloging-in-Publication Data

Brandt, Jennifur.
   Life is a movie starring you : the pesky meddling girls guide to living your dreams / by Jennifur Brandt.
      p. cm.
   ISBN 0-446-67633-0
   1. Teenage girls--Conduct of life. I. Title.

BJ1651 .B73 2000
646.7'00835'2--dc21

00-039900

To these People I send Pink champagne Wishes and glitter lip-gloss Kisses

My Pesky mom Moira . . . if i'm the princess of the Pesky Meddling Empire then you're the Queen, My Pesky dad Larry for believing in me even when I had a Mohawk and making all my dreams come true, Lizzie for being my Pesky Meddling muse . . . I will never listen to Heart or "Jenny and the Jet's" without thinking of you, Randolph for that inspirational chat on Melanie's couch and for 'blinding me with science', My glam editor and Pesky cheerleader Caryn Karmatz Rudy who has been my guide in turning life into a movie, Larry Kirshbaum for saying "yes" and promises of Karaoke nights to come, Michael Harkavy for escorting me on my heroes journey, Karen Weiss for believing first, Greg Homer for your brilliance, Michelle Sucillon for your support and general Pesky-ness, Diane Luger & the art dept. for making the cover so de-voom, Torrey Oberfest & her proofreading posse, Anna Sui and Thomas, Drew B. and Chris, Karen McTier, Mr. Benchley, Doug Little, all my furrends & family, and every Pesky girl on this glammy planet!

Contents

About the Author

Jennifur Brandt was born smack dab in the heart of Hollywood. Her family knew something was weird when all her grandma's false eyelashes kept disappearing. When she was a preteen, dreams of becoming an editrix for *Vogue* were all a-swirl in her head . . . so in junior high she started her own Xeroxed fanzine called *Pesky Meddling Girls*. Word of lipsticked mouth spread quickly about the wacky girly 'zine and soon after stars were subscribing left and right. Anna Sui asked Jennifur to design collaged tee shirts for two of her collections, *Hard Copy* followed her around on a shopping spree for vintage frocks, she was crowned 'Zine Queen in the premier issue of *Teen People*, and a casting agent gave her the coveted part in the classic film *Clueless* as "the nosejob girl," But she knew her dreams had come true when god of all glam rock . . . Mr. David Bowie, called for an ish. Jennifur now resides with her family (including her cat Tallulah, the Pesky Meddling Mascot), in The Valley . . . which she finds to be a totally tubular setting for her Pesky Meddling Empire.

2

✶ **Meet the Pesky Photographess** ✶

Lizzie Brandt was the youngest girl *ever* to be hired as a photographer for *Teen People* magazine. In the premier issue, no less! She shoots every cover of my 'zine (*Pesky Meddling Girls*), and has studied photography at both Oxford and Art Center. In her spare time she designs her own clothes using tacky fabrics from the '70s, daydreams about living in New York City (whilst wearing a Danskin leotard like in *Fame,*) and becoming a music video director. Today my sis' is twenty-one and resides in San Francisco, where she lives in a rockin' art deco apartment (of which I am sooo jealous). Lizzie is one of us . . . a girly girl who goes after her dreams.

About our Pesky Meddling Illustrator . . .

Erika Pahk and I first met when she became a subscriber to my 'zine. She would write me letters on homemade stationery covered in her fun sketches of fashiony girls. I flipped over her extraordinary talent. So, when the fab publishing fairies called, VOILA! . . . I knew Erika was my girl. **She is only seventeen**, and is inspired by the following; old movies, '70s punk music, Twiggy, Audrey Hepburn, and her furrends. This Pesky Girls dreams for the future are; working for Anna Sui, attending an artsy college, and becoming a famous costume designer à-la Edith Head. Enjoy her de-voomly gorgeous illustrations and let her be a teen inspiration to you all.

P.esky **S**.ecret: When you see her initials (*ekp*) you'll know it's an original Erika Pahk work of genius.

Your Purrsonal Info Page *

"Whooooo are Yoooooooo?"—The Cheshire Cat   Today's date:

Full name and nickname:

Address:

Phone number: Your best friend's phone number:

Birthday: Birthplace:

Astrological sign:

Hair color (at the moment):   Eye color:

The colors that make you happy are . . .

Which animal best represents your purrsonality?

Where do you hang out on the weekends?

Your inspirational motto or mantra is . . .

Write a little poem about yourself:

Glue your fave photograph of yourself here:

4

Use this page to write about whatever comes to mind. Don't censor yourself, just write stream of conciousness-style . . . 1 . . . 2 . . . 3 . . . GO!

_____
_____
_____
_____
_____
_____
_____
_____
_____
_____
_____
_____
_____
_____
_____
_____
_____
_____
_____
_____
_____
_____
_____
_____
_____
_____

A Note from Your Director

Kitten . . . here's a secret that will change your sparkly life forever. It's a magical mantra that came to me in a dream one night, which is where my snazziest artsy notions usually pop up . . . in dreams, or, to be honest . . . on the loo, but I won't go there. Baby doll, you better embroider *this* on your psychedelic pillow in glitter thread . . . "Life Is a Movie Starring You", and don't you forget it! I was directionless and introverted before I had this delicious revelation. I chant this mantra every morning even before washing off my sticky mascara from the evening before. It awakens the truly Pesky Girl living inside my shy heart, and I promise it will do the same for you. When you chant "Life is a movie starring ME," what you are really saying is "Screw reality!" So what if you have PMS pimples, and your sister finagled your fave dress without a permission slip . . . your boy toy turned out to be a major jerk, and your tummy goes beyond belly dancer . . . so what? This life is your damn MOVIE . . . and nobody else's . . . you've got alot of other jazz to worry about. After all you are the director, writer, music coordinator, costumer . . . and, most of all, **star!**

Life Is a Movie Starring YOU . . . Dahhling!

Now that you're in the right spirit, we've got work to do. I want you to take a good, hard look at your movie . . . Does your script need a few rewrites? Does it have a really great plot, with not too much drama? Does it make people laugh? Is it witty? Is the costuming kicking butt? And, most important, is it rated PG? (Pesky Girl, of course . . .) Once you've caught a glimpse of your own story line, roll up those sequined sleeves, roll out that imaginary red carpet, and remember that it is within your Pesky Princess power to give each day a happy ending. Get ready for your closeup!

Love & glitter lip-gloss kisses,

Jennifer

⭐ "What Is a Pesky ⭐ Meddling Girl?"

Before you can begin to evaluate your Pesky movie, you may be wondering what being Pesky is all about! Well, cats and kittens, here's the scoop:

⭐ A Pesky Meddling Girl is definitely outspoken, but never rude.

⭐ She loves the past, yet looks forward to the future.

⭐ She's all about glam—and she's glam in everything from sparkly vintage gowns to faded jeans and a Blondie concert tee.

⭐ She is open-minded and has pin-up girl-confidence.

⭐ She loves to read and educate herself and values all culture.

⭐ She is Gidget meets Christina Ricci.

⭐ She is both Cyndi Lauper & Twiggy.

⭐ She is That Girl & everygirl.

⭐ She is, in short . . . YOU!

Have doubts? Don't worry, every word on these pink (and yellow and blue) pages is designed to help you get to know your Pesky self. It is a rockin' fantasy book in which you will record all your heart's deepest desires, all the stuff you've been dying to ditch, and get inspiration for all that creative energy you've been storing up inside. By the end of this book, you'll feel so foxy, you'll want to throw a huge soiree in your own honor—and if they're Pesky enough . . . your friends will clamor to RSVP.

⭐ Don't forget to chant your Pesky mantra as you get dolled up:

"LIFE IS A MOVIE STARRING ME!"

Getting Into Character

Who are you really? And who do you WANT to be? Sometimes you find yourself stuck in a movie that's just plain dullsville because the characters don't feel real to you. This can happen when you are struggling to be a copycat character just like all the others you see around you. But it doesn't have to be that way. Take, for example, Old-Fashioned Moi . . .

Old-Fashioned Moi

I've been nostalgic for the past since I can remember . . . which was around the age of five. My parents began acknowledging my weirdness when I faked a flu in the third grade so I could secretly watch my Mom's VHS copy of *Gone With the Wind*. I had been dying to see more of the foofy hoop skirts and flowery décolletage displayed by the revelatory Vivien Leigh on the cover. I popped it in and from the second she sighs "fiddle dee dee" in that Southern meow of an accent, I was hooked. She was astonishing . . . the purest essence of girlhood. I watched the four-hour flick twice, in one day no less. I've always been obsessed with the past. Maybe it's that people just seemed more polite and courteous, followed a clear code of ethics (excluding the '60s through the '80s of course), and wore swankier clothes. I love to romance the notion of what my life might have been like if I had lived in another time and place (not to Shirley MacLaine out or anything). I guess I'll always be an old-fashioned girl.

And even though I was an eight-year-old weirdo playing hooky to watch *Gone With the Wind*, I embraced my weirdness! All my friends would've said, "Old movies are so boring . . . let's go to Raging Waters" (some hygienically gross water park in San Dimas, made famous by *Bill & Ted's Excellent Adventure*). But whilst they were busy scraping their butts on all the water slides, and getting beamed in the skulls by boogie boards in the wave pool . . . I was giving myself a Pesky education in culture. I may have seemed out of step, but I was making myself happy. Not that there's anything wrong with pool hopping, but if you much prefer the "Boogie Woogie Bugle Boy" to boogie boards, then you must follow your own tune. If a friend attempts to make you feel superlame or overly studious for wanting to make yourself smarter, silently plot your future revenge — start plotting *your* film . . . one more epic than *Gone With the Wind* could ever be: The Story of {your name here}.

ekp

Are you an old-fashioned gal? If so, how? *Pesky Pencil*

_____
_____

Of course, not everyone grooves to a retro beat. What counts is that you figure out what is YOU. Without a clear sense of your character, moviemaking can get muddled, so here's a list of questions to start you off on establishing your charmingly kooky character du jour.

List all the reasons why you rock: _____
_____
_____

List everything that makes you different from other girls: _____
_____

Who and what do you love with all your heart? _____
_____
_____
_____

What makes you laugh? _____
What are you afraid of? _____
Where do you find spirituality: _____
_____
_____

If you had access to a time machine, what year would you visit, and why? _____
_____
_____
_____

My Pesky/Poopy List

One way to understand your sparkly star self better is to measure ideas, people, fashion, and anything you have an opinion about on a **Pesky/Poopy** scale. Here's mine:

Pesky

- sparkly tiaras
- board game parties
- hot cherry pie
- Karaoke
- go-go dancing
- Drew Barrymore
- Friday night movie dates
- freckles
- Manhattan
- getting e-mail and snail mail
- my cats . . . Tallulah & Petita
- faux fur
- *Behind the Music* on VH1
- chocolate malts
- my disco ball
- orchid & vanilla incense

drew B. drawn by me!

meow

Petita

yummy

Poopy

- cigarettes
- PMS pimples
- being bitchy to other girls
- following trends
- post-donut guilt
- getting drunk
- process of growing out bangs
- when my boudoir is messy
- cruelty to animals
- nervous stomachaches
- stupid sitcoms
- tall men in front of me at the movies
- people who don't recycle

Your Pesky/Poopy List:

Go ahead, list everything you adore and abhor

Pesky

Poopy

CINEMASCOOP! It's me, in Hollywood! Going to the movies in my fave vintage gown.

CINEMASCOOP

"I've always wanted two lives—one for the movies, one for myself." —Greta Garbo

PESKY MEDDLING MOVIES YOU MUST RENT

A true Pesky Meddling Girl seeks character inspiration from the glittering silver screen. Women to admire and adore are just a play button away.

CLUELESS—It's me in my big screen debut! Look for me itching my faux nosejob cast with a cell phone antenna.

AUNTIE MAME—You've never seen real elaborately glam costuming until you've seen this. Her motto is "Life is a Banquet," and she is one truly Pesky siren. This film has changed my life, as well as my set decor.

PAPER MOON—Tatum O'Neil is a feisty kid on the run with her sweet scamp father. She won a Best Actress Oscar for this role at the ripe ol' age of nine!

SIXTEEN CANDLES—The first in a trio of films by genius director John Hughes starring his muse Molly Ringwald. She is my fave '80s flapper . . . the teen queen of pink & pout.

GENTLEMEN PREFER BLONDES—Marilyn Monroe and Jane Russell are my buxom goddesses. Based on the brilliant book written by Anita Loos in the '20s.

XANADU—Be inspired by the eternal roller skating muse that is Olivia Newton-John. Ooh-la-la pink leg-warmers galore, and a dreamy soundtrack by ELO.

THE WOMEN—Features Joan Crawford, Paulette Goddard, Roz Russell, other sirens, sequins, and many layers of tulle!

VALLEY GIRL—"She's cool. He's hot. She's from the valley. He's not." Starring a like, totally tubular Nicolas Cage, and my fave mall . . . The Sherman Oaks Galleria, okay?

IT—This silent gem stars the very first It Girl herself, Clara Bow. It's the cat's meow, dollface!

BUGSY MALONE—Fab Jodie Foster stars as a flapper named Tallulah. I named my kitty (the Pesky mascot) after her.

pretty in pink—MY #1 FAVORITE FILM OF ALL TIME!

Molly Ringwald is the pure essence of Pesky in this film. Words cannot describe to you how much this film has influenced my art, my life, and how much pink there is in my closet! I know you will hail it as the be-all-end-all '80s teen classic. It's all about US!

Molly Ringwald by Jennifer

"*Movie Queen*"

it's marilyn!

Roman Holiday—Audrey plays a princess who goes AWOL in order to see Rome, and falls in true love with Gregory Peck during her swanky adventure.

Ladies and Gentlemen, The Fabulous Stains—Featuring an all-grrrl punk band whose mantra is "We're the Stains! And we don't put out!."

Gone With the Wind—Vivien Leigh as Scarlett O'Hara. Need I say more?

The Scarlet Empress—Marlene Dietrich rules as the last empress of Russia.

Three Smart Girls—Thirteen-year-old opera singer Deanna Durbin is the true meaning of girl power! F.Y.I., This film saved Universal Studios from bankruptcy.

The Girl Can't Help It!—Jayne Mansfield va-va-vooms across the silver screen in the first all Rock & Roll 1950s flick, and her greatest purrformance.

JAYNE MANSFIELD

AUDREY HEPBURN

Breakfast at Tiffany's—The girliest movie ever made. I'm actually speechless about it. Audrey Hepburn is a revelation as the character Holly Golightly. Also featuring killer costuming by Givenchy.

Say Anything . . .—John Cusack (did I forget to tell you he's my husband?) swoonfully stars as the archetypal Pesky boyfriend. Sigh . .

Entertainment

Grease—Pink ladies and poodle skirts, beauty school dropouts, and hotties in hot rods. Learn to hand jive with Olivia Newton-John and John Travolta.

Queen Christina—GARBO, Garbo, and more genius Garbo!

The Boy Friend—Twiggy stars and shines in this 1970s style-fest about 1920s vaudeville actors. I decorated my boudoir based on the bohemian vibe of the sets.

Buffalo 66—Watch Christina Ricci beam brilliance at you from every pore. Warning! May cause you to enroll in tap dancing school.

Calamity Jane—She's the rootin'est tootin'est cowgirl around! Starring cutesy-pie Doris Day.

★ Coal Miner's Daughter—Y'all better go see Sissy Spacek as honky-tonk queen Loretta Lynn, or i'll send ya' straight to fist city!

Hairspray—A teen Ricki Lake rounds up all her "hair-hopper" friends to fight against segregation, whilst Twisting the night away.

Cleopatra Jones—A dark and lovely diva fights crime in 1970s L.A. whilst sporting an Afro and huge platforms. I call her look kung-fu couture. Git down!

Funny Face—Charming Audrey Hepburn stars as a jazzy beatnik/bookworm who reluctantly becomes a model, and falls in love with her photographer (Fred Astaire) while posing. S'wonderful!

Rushmore—A masterpiece of Pesky cinema! Teens in the '60s had Dustin Hoffman as *The Graduate*, and we've got rockin'-genius Jason Schwartzman as Max Fischer.

The Gidget Trilogy—See all three: *Gidget*, *Gidget Goes to Rome*, and *Gidget Goes Hawaiian*. Sandra Dee + Moondoggie 4-ever.

Pesky

List all the flicks you'd recommend I rent: _____
_____
_____
_____
_____

Your all-time fave flick is: _____

What scene in a film deeply inspired or touched you? _____
_____

Your fave actresses & actors are . . . _____
_____
_____

If a film was being made of your life, who would play you? _____

The title of the film would be . . . _____

The plot would go like this . . . _____
_____

PESKY POP QUIZ:

A film frenzied friend invites you to see America's first silent sweetheart, Mary Pickford, starring in a movie marathon at your local artsy theater. You've never seen a silent film before. You . . .

★ **A.** Assume all silent movies are boring and opt for renting *American Pie* instead.

★ **B.** Aren't quite sure if you'll end up in Snoozville, so you take your own car.

★ **C.** Are totally gung ho for trying something new, and are sure that after the film you'll be corkscrew-curling your hair and thinking that talkies are just a fad.

If you circled C (okay, and B too!), then you are a true Pesky film nerd!
That is the highest honor to be bestowed upon any girl starring in her own movie!

Still worried you don't have star quality? Here are some tips for building up all the confidence you need to star in your own movie.

Funny Face—When someone laughs at you . . . the best thing to do is to laugh with them. Being funny is a gift . . . famous comedians pay big moolah to gag writers for the natural gift you possess. It means you are like a modern Lucille Ball. My lil' sis' Lizzie used to cry buckets when the kids at school would crack up at her kookiness . . . until I taught her that being the center of attention at every recess meant that she had a natural magnetism, which made people want to watch her. After all, school wouldn't be any fun without the class clown. Lizzie now realizes that almost all the boys who teased her in fifth grade, really had designs on her. If you have a talent for entertaining effortlessly . . . roll with it, funny girl! You should start a career with all that star quality.

"Tomorrow is another day."—Scarlett O'Hara—Have an inspirational mantra ready to get you or a friend through a sucky day. My beau's fave thing to say to me when I'm feeling blue is "It'll all be better in the morning." . . . and then there is that one which has been so super-inspirational to me . . . "Life is a movie starring you." So pick your fave mantra, and embroider it in pink ribbon on your mental pillow.

Carry a journal or scrapbook in your purse at all times—It will give you a secret place to write your purrsonal thoughts at any time of the day. You can also glue lil' souvenirs from places you've been . . . not to mention that it looks all hip and beatniky to whip one out. People will think you are some renowned poet like Jack Kerouac.

List all of your lucky charms: _____

_____

Write me a letter! Send it to: Jennifur, The Pesky Meddling Girl

c/o Warner Books, 1271 Avenue of the Americas, New York, NY 10020

P.esky **S.**ecret: *I'm a really good pen pal.*

Jenny's final thought—You can't change your entire demeanor overnight, unless you wiggle your nose à la Tabitha on *Bewitched*. It's gonna take some thought and practice to dump those naughty words, nasty ways, and be able to purr "Hello, gorgeous" to the new you. Just be patient. Now go on! . . . Become the smash hit of your very own Technicolor creation!

Casting Call

Imagine, hypothetically for a moment, if Paramount Pictures had chosen Marilyn Monroe to play the legendary role of Holly Golightly, instead of Audrey Hepburn, in the flick *Breakfast at Tiffany's*. The result would've been amusing, yes, but most surely would've stunk. She would've been wrongly cast as a gamine socialite. Or picture a scene from *Clueless*—but instead of Alicia Silverstone's sunny portrayal of Cher, envision Christina Ricci in her ultra-goth *Addams Family* days. What you would then have is a totally different movie.

The point is, your cast is one of the most crucial components of your movie—they should enhance your performance, deepen your character, and make you feel great about yourself. And no matter how pretty on paper a cast may seem, it is the chemistry that counts—those that glitter on the outside but are actually dull and thoughtless equal an instant box office bomb! Do you know what you are looking for in a friend? Here are some of my fave movie pals with characteristics I prize in real friends. I'm using characters from my fave flicks **Pretty in Pink** {*the* Pesky-est film of all time} and **Grease** {another classic} as examples, so if you haven't seen these flicks yet, please put this book down and go rent them immediately! Just kidding . . . you'll catch my drift, don't worry. On with the show . . .

Your Cast

FRENCHY—Everybody needs a best girl friend. In *Grease*, she was Sandy's, and I'm sure yours is just as cool. One night at a pep rally, French (as her girl-gang The Pink Ladies called her) witnessed drag-racing hottie Danny Zuko acting like a jerk to her best friend Sandy, so to cheer Sandy up . . . she gave her a va-va-voom makeover. This sweet "beauty school dropout" did everything in her pink-haired power to restore her friend's happiness. Every girl needs a friend like Frenchy . . . one who is devoted to you and who is always considerate of your feelings. You should feel like family around each other. Make an effort not to act selfish . . . Pesky example: If you promised her you'd help her study for an exam, and some guy asks you out for that same eve, you would never dream of flaking on her . . . that is what a strong friendship is all about. A best friend is someone who, like you, is generous and who helps you to be the star of your own movie. But here's the Pesky rub . . . to have a fab best friend, you have to *be* a fab best friend. I've always tried to picture what happens to the girls after *Grease* ends and the cast is all waving 'bye to Danny and Sandy as they drive away in his hot rod, Greased Lightning . . . I bet she goes off with Danny to Blueberry Hill for a couple of smoocheroos, then runs directly to the mall, where she meets Frenchy, and they gossip, try on tight pencil skirts so they can attempt to be as cool as Rizzo (leader of The Pink Ladies), and rate Danny's kisses, while sipping chocolate milkshakes. Cut and print . . .

If you haven't found your dream Frenchy yet, don't despair, she's out there somewhere, and it's just like finding a beau . . . you always meet them when you'd least expect it. I'm still searching for mine.

My sister Lizzie looks for the following qualities in a Frenchy:

"They'd have to be someone strange and interesting, with endearing qualities. We have different interests, but want to learn about each other's. She inspires me to do things with my life, whereas other people just kind of drain me."

♥ List here ALL your very bestest friends:

_____

_____

_____

_____

_____

_____

_____

A pic of my cute Pesky sister Lizzie and my de-voomly gorgeous mom, Moira.

List all the reasons why *your* Frenchy is so very Pesky: _____

_____

If you don't have one yet, list the qualities you'd like her to have: _____

_____

This is a page to have your Frenchy fill out about you!
So create a special questionnaire just for her:

If you are at a loss for Pesky questions, here are some fun ones I thought of . . . ✳What is your name, nickname, and astrological sign? ✳What's your inspirational motto? ✳What's the funniest sitch we've been in together? ✳What is your purrsonal Pesky message to me? Anyway . . . channel your inner Barbara Walters, and ask away, dollface!

YOUR DUCKIE—Duckie is the purrfect boy character to describe your bestest, yet purely platonic, boy friend. He's almost better than any beau, because you are free to love him with all your heart, yet there's no drama involved because you don't want to snog (British slang for kiss) him. Flashing yellow light: Even if there is no drama on your end, he may have some on his. When in the presence of such a dazzling creature as yourself, how can you not expect him to fall in crush with you? He's your adoring fan, for the good performances and for the bad ones, too. And if he's a good Duckie, he'll even stick by your side through boyfriends (gay best-boyfriends are sometimes better at dealing with this particular sitch, but anyway . . .) In case you do happen to notice a warm glowy vibe emitting from his eyes whenever he looks at you, or you happen to smell the ashes from his smouldering heart . . . be sure to sit him down and let him know exactly how important his friendship is to you, and how you wouldn't want *anything* to ruin it. Another thing you should try not to do with a guy pal who's secretly crushin' on you is to spend too much psuedo-date-esque time together. Boys get confused easily and misinterpret our naturally intriguing ways. Maybe you could even try to set up your Duckman with a girl deserving of his adoration . . . I know it'll be hard to see your biggest flatterer light his torch someplace new, but he'll be happy, and he'll still want to hang with you. Remember . . . a good friend is not selfish. Duckies are like our fuzziest blanket . . . warm and around for life. They are the boys we never kiss, yet probably should've. Ducksters always know the right thing to say to make *you* feel Pretty in Pink.

Who is your Duckie? _____

Name any Duckies that you're diggin' as potential beau material: _____

_____

Be a Pal . . .

(Pronounced: eye·ohh·nah)

IONA—(Pronounced: eye·ohh·nah) Poor Andi Walsh (Molly Ringwald's character in *Pretty in Pink*) . . . she had been horribly dumped by the preppie of her dreams, on the day of her senior prom! Her entire life was thrown into turmoil. Not only was she treated like the plague by the pop girls, but she had also lost her Duckie (after he had been in crush with her his whole life,) by agreeing to attend the prom with a trust-fund baby named Blane. What was she to do? Go home and weep her gownless self to sleep whilst listening to sad records by The Smiths? She needed serious guidance, advice from a girl who had seen it all before, so she hopped in her pink Karmann Ghia and drove right over to the retro pad of the wickedly fashionable Iona.

Iona may have been her boss at the record shop, Traxx, where Andi was cashier, but age had no bearing on the situation because they shared a bond. Andi reminded Iona of herself when she was a teen, and I'm sure Andi wanted to grow up to be just as rockin' as Iona . . . this is how a mentorship begins. A mentor is someone who is usually older than you, with more life experience. A mentor is someone you aspire to be. This friendship differs from the relationship you have with your Frenchy, because your bestest girl friend is someone you are experiencing life with as it happens, when everything is totally new to you both . . . whereas an Iona can help you to get through things with minimal drama due to the fact that she's already covered that scene. Anyone you look up to, respect, and hope to be as cool as when you're their age, can be a mentor.

I've had a couple of Iona's in my life . . . one I remember was a girl named Karen that used to baby-sit my sister & me in the '80s. She was in junior high, so we looked up to her as if she were a goddess. The words she spoke were like our holy grail. She taught me things I'll never forget, like . . . "Vintage clothes are better than new ones because they have history." She was a Pesky inspiration to me, and I always tried really hard to act "mature" around her. But when I turned eighteen I found my coolest, and current mentor, my mom! I was such a brat to her all through my teens, and then I realized just how cool she is. She's unlike any mom I've met, and I'll strive to be as cool as her when I'm pushin' fifty (she'll *kill* me for writing that). My mom just "gets it". She has flaming red hair, which she wears in Pippi Longstocking braids, a face like Debbie Harry, and she goes to work wearing vintage Chinese pajamas. She cares not what anyone else thinks of her, even though she pretends she does for modesty's sake. She believes that you should always try to display who you truly are. She keeps my entire family in check and dispenses guru-esque advice to all my friends. In fact, they sometimes call her and don't even ask for me! She's passionate about living, and these are all the reasons she's *my* Iona.

Who is your Iona? _____

What in particular is mentor-ific about that purrson? _____

_____

List everyone who's inspirational to you & why:

_____   _____
_____   _____
_____   _____
_____   _____
_____   _____
_____   _____
_____   _____
_____   _____
_____   _____
_____   _____
_____   _____
_____   _____
_____   _____
_____   _____

When you are an Iona, what piece of wisdom will you pass on to another Pesky girl?

_____

List all the people (dead or alive, famous or not) **you'd love to have a Pesky chat with over a chocolate milkshake:**

_____
_____
_____
_____
_____
_____

SOMETIMES, IT CAN FEEL LIKE THERE ISN'T AN IONA, DUCKIE, OR FRENCHY TO BE FOUND. I'VE BEEN THERE. DON'T WORRY . . . THEY'LL APPEAR WHEN YOU LEAST EXPECT IT.

What to Do When You Are Panned by Your Critics

Let me tell you a little ol' fact I've discovered about being popular and thoroughly accepted in school, and in life . . . If you are the perfect teen, with perfect skin, who has a perfect figure, everyone adores, and isn't even given given a curfew by your parents, 'cuz you are *always* home at a reasonable hour, and your grades are magically perfect, and Elite models wants to represent you, but you're gonna wait till after Yale, then, my dearest girl . . . I feel sorry for you . . . 'cuz unfortunately, you have peaked. As a girl I think it rocks to have a hard time in school. I wouldn't have traded my "Square Peg" years for a bod like Naomi Campbell. Us dorks seemed to be having a lot more fun anyway. We were more free, and had no image to uphold. We didn't judge each other. Being tortured in public drags you through hell and out the other side. Without difficult experiences, and the feeling of being an outsider, what would we have to draw back on when we are in need of any inspiration, artistic or otherwise? When you are Miss Perfecto in high school, whilst everyone else is hating life, then those years will probably turn out to have been the best ones of your life. When you have to go out into the crazy lightning-paced world, nobody is gonna make you homecoming queen, you have to be the one to crown yourself and know how to truly let others' opinions roll off your tiara. Cherish all the years you feel like a freak on a daily basis, get lost in your thoughts and dreams about the future, because I promise that when you 100% ignore others' mistreatment of lil' ol' you, the world will look like a much Pesky-er planet, with infinite possibilities to create something all YOU. Remember . . . nobody can make you feel like a dork without your consent. When an out-of-touch critic bashes a flick you've been dying to see all year, do you piggybank your eight bucks . .

or do you dismiss it as his own farty opinion, not yours, and break out the Raisinets anyway? . . . Thought so.

PESKY THINGS TO DO:

★ Instead of joining a clique . . . try being a floater. This way people won't be intimidated by you, and won't make assumptions that you are exactly like the rest of your "gang." You'll make more friends, and have the freedom to hang in different circles with no drama involved.

If I were a bumblebee I would sting these UN-PESKY people: _____

_____

List every nickname you've been given (the sweet ones, and the sour): _____

_____

ekp

"It's better to be looked over than overlooked." —Mae West

Be Adored by the Critics

To put it as best I can, dahhling . . . just remember to **be yourself!** and if that takes a little soul searching, so be it. If there is a gang of kids you would love to join, and they are snubbing you by making it hard to get to know them in any way, then these are the wrong friends for you. Finding the ones who you will "clique" with should be effortless and low maintenance. They will accept you for who you are. It took me forever to find my dreamy soul mate friends, and they were the people I'd least expect. They just showed up at a party, and we all dug being together, no effort involved. I think when I was in school I tried too hard to impress the friends I had. I did not give them the gift of knowing the real me, and I think kids can sense that about you. In school I did have my "cast," but it never felt quite natural. What I probably should've been doing instead of hanging out with them at Denny's most nights, was taking some time to get to know myself. Take as much time as you need to figure out exactly who that glammy goddess of self-love is . . . just take a deep breath, and start to envision what kind of a girl you'd like to be . . . Would you like to be perceived as artsy, witty, an honest friend, a Renaissance girl, eccentric, optimistic, life of the soiree, debutante, evil bad grrrl?

Make a list here of some qualities you'd like to work on developing inside yourself, so you are that much closer to being your very own dream girl:

_____

_____

_____

_____

_____

_____

_____

_____

"Each one of us is a brain and an athlete, a basket case, a princess and a criminal."

—Anthony Michael Hall
In The Breakfast Club

In what ways are you are a rockin' friend to have:

_____

_____

_____

What games do you dig playing with your posse?

_____

What was the most thoughtful gift you have ever recieved?

a_____from _____

What was the most thoughtful gift you have ever given?

a_____given to_____

You and your friends are going to start an exclusive club called
The Pesky Meddling Girls. What are the membership rules? _____

_____

_____

_____

Where will Pesky headquarters be? _____

What will you do when you meet?   _____

_____

_____

_____

_____

✵ PESKY THiNGS TO DO:

➜ Throw a board-game party for your friends one Friday night instead of going out.

➜ Tell your boy toy once in a while that you are busy on Saturday night. Ask your best gal pal, sister, or your mom out for a movie date. Be sure to have girly-bonding over some junky food (Pringles, Cocoa Puffs, and Raisinets would be my pics.)

➜ Befriend a major nerd at school, but DON'T give them a makeover. DO embrace them in all their goofy glory.

24 Dealing with *
* Your Agents

An agent's relationship to a movie star is that of advisor, protector, and guardian. They make sure the celeb is making all the right career as well as life decisions. They are sometimes mentors and dispense caring advice when it's needed. In your case . . . your agents are your parents, or whoever has your life's best interests at heart. Sometimes, if a Hollywood agent's client starts acting childish, making unreasonable demands, insisting on only shooting films with undesirable co-stars, gathering tons of bad press along the way, resulting in films that flop, the agent no longer supports his or her client. That is what could happen with you and your 'rents, if you don't behave like a real sweet glamour puss at least on occasion.

I know some of you may not have the best parents (or as we call them in Hollywood, "players'") in the business, but you make do with the cards fate has dealt you. The smart thing is to keep stressful confrontations at a minimum. I went through it all, believe moi. Imagine growing up in Hollywood . . . with temptation to be bad all around you. I was getting invites from celebrity schoolmates to go clubbing with them till dawn, and this was when I was nine! I went to slumber parties in the hills above Sunset Blvd. in my preteen years where the *parents* were offering me joints! Pressure to hang with the cool crowd here is brutal, and I wouldn't suggest it for any young girl, especially one that is ultra-dorky and comes from an extremely strict family, like I did.

List all the cool things about your agents: _____

_____

_____

What character traits have you inherited from them?

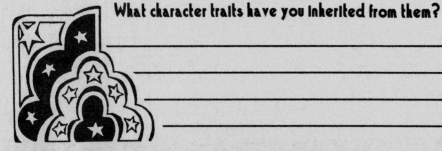

When I turned sixteen everything went downhill for my protective agents and me. I was sick of always being the nerdy one . . . the prudelike Goody Two-shoes, so I started to instigate screaming fights with my dad to let me go out with the bad friends I wanted to, and to extend my curfew on school nights. (This was necessary for me since none of my friends even knew the meaning of the word *curfew*.) I did everything in my power to rebel against them . . . shaving my head into a neon red Mohawk, piercing my eyebrow and nose with safety pins, flunking classes, and acting ridiculously melodramatic and immature. I eventually ran away, with my black vinyl hat box fully filled with the necessities for surviving on the streets . . . a cassette by Siouxsie & the Banshees, a Ziploc bag of quarters, pointy witch boots with bat buckles up the side, and a velvet cape. Being the sheltered chicken that I was . . . I got as far as the stop sign on my corner, then sat there until my mom told me to get back in the house.

Looking back on my utter drama queen-ness, and my throwing the entire house into stressy turmoil . . . it's probably the one thing I really regret about my teen time. My parents and I never really came to an understanding during those years, but as I got a little fed up with myself, and one by one my merely bad friends became total degenerates and delinquents, I really noticed how hard my parents had tried all those years to keep me safe. They just kept putting in the effort to show me that they loved me. We've since put all our emotions out on the table about those times, and talked about how hard those years were for me as well. The coolest thing is . . . now I LIKE them and dig hanging out with them. What brought about the change? I guess I just woke up one day and felt like a little poop about all I'd put them through . . .

This revelation hit me really hard the day I learned that my dad had cancer. I had thought of my dad only as superman before that . . . he was healthy and seemed invincible to me. I had to watch him become pale, bald, and vulnerable. His illness changed my perspective thoroughly. I wanted to be a truly good-hearted person, and love my family regardless of our differences and petty disagreements. Life is too short, and if my dad hadn't survived his sick days, I would've never been able to forgive myself for how much unnecessary heartache I'd given him.

It pays to take the time to work things out in a mature manner. Spend more time getting to know your parents; they were once your age too, and most likely understand your frustrations. Sometimes they don't react the way you expect them to when you ask for a change in the house rules, not because they want you to hate them or to cause a fight, but because they'd die inside if anything bad happened to you. And if you request a later curfew, to no avail, then do what I should've done . . . come home on time and work on creating something artistic, watch some good movies on cable, anything . . . just don't waste all your energy fighting, it's such an ugly thing to do, and it causes premature wrinkles as well. Your family is the cast you cannot choose, they are already under contract . . . so try and make every day on the set a pleasant and enjoyable one.

During which childhood moment did you feel the most lucky? _____

26 _____

What important values has your family instilled in you? _____

_____

On what occasion did you most bond with your agents? _____

_____

The time you were most busted by your 'rents for being naughty was . . . _____

_____

When you become an agent yourself, what will you name your little stars? _____

_____

Draw a family tree. Include all your fave Pesky relatives:

How to become a mover and a shaker in your agents' eyes:

✳ Remember that the only way to have your agents truly accept you and your choices in life . . . is to accept them & their choices. After all, dollface . . . acceptance is a two-way street. Here you can observe how a Pesky point of view can make annoying situations more bearable . . .

✳ Since you *are* the center of the universe . . . why not give all your devoted fans a chance to be in your presence. There is plenty of time to play with your friends, so try to schedule in some time for your family. Trust me . . . they'll be thrilled!

✳ There is one group of people that almost every kid and her parents can agree on, and that's . . . The Beatles. Plan one hour a week when the whole family eats dessert together and listens to a different Beatles album . . . Dance, talk, and bond over their brilliance.

✳ Don't be a bitchy queen of sarcasm to the parental unit. They love you, so try to be nice.

✳ Experiment with telling the truth . . . and let them know that you're on an honesty trip.

✳ LAST DITCH RESORT—If you see a pattern in your agents' way of dealing with things that goes against what you believe in . . . instead of fighting with them about it, keep it in mind for when you have children so you won't make the same mistakes. Sometimes they are giving you an education in how *not* to raise children, and if you're astute enough to notice it, then most likely you'll be a fab parent when it gets to be your time up at bat.

Things you should try to say to your agents more often:
✳ Good Morning ✳ I'm home! ✳ please ✳ thank you ✳ I'm sorry

Make a list of three parental habits that bug you, and then make an effort to change your attitude about just one:

_____

_____

_____

_____

Dealing with your Costars

Laverne has Shirley . . . Lorelei Lee has Dorothy . . . Cher has Dionne . . . I have Lizzie. I was three years old when my mom gave birth to what I viewed as a setback in my plan of being my parents' only fairy princess angel baby. I would now be forced to share my Barbies, trade in my pink canopy lounge for a bunk bed, and wear matching dresses with someone who was drooling. Needless to say, Lizzie and I hit some rough patches on the long & winding road to teendom. We gave the word *brat* a whole new meaning. I think Damien (otherwise known as *The Omen*) would've peed his pants at how evil my sister and I were to each other.

From the moment she learned how how to speak, she had perfected the art of blaming everything on me, which usually resulted in some amateur ninjitsu tournaments. She was also a mastermind at blackmail. An example of one of her schemes is this . . . "If you don't give me your Pee Wee's Playhouse Colorforms, I will bite myself until I bleed and say you did it!" I called her bluff on enough occasions to know that she would always go through with it, and inevitably I'd end up grounded for a week. We became more and more like Aaron Spelling/*Dynasty*-esque villains as the years went by . . . pulling each other's braids, and hurting each other's feelings using our most beloved passions as bait (ex.: "David Hasselhoff will NEVER marry you!"). Yet show me a pair of sisters who've never wanted to kill each other, and I'll show you two robots in long wigs.

Age difference is always the issue. It makes you natural rivals. I mean, when she was in seventh grade and literally weeping over the New Kids on the Block, I was in my bedroom writing "meat is murder" on my arm with a Sharpie . . . we were the more-than-odd couple, the teenybopper and the punk rocker. So, after nineteen years of reluctantly sharing a bathroom, phone line, and parental attention . . . Lizzie moved to San Francisco to attend college. I got my wish! I have the whole setup to myself. I no longer find my fave date dress mysteriously missing from my closet. I don't have to bang on the bathroom door while she does her makeup for three hours. I always get shotgun when I ride in the car with Mom. Yet I always feel like a piece of me is missing. I'm always a little bit sad. It wasn't until she moved away that I realized she was my best friend. Who knows me better than her? Who has been there every time I've cried? I wouldn't trade all those years in hormonal combat for anything in the world.

ekp

Through Thick and Thin

I interviewed LIZZIE on her thoughts about older brothers and sisters and how they should treat the babies of the family:

You have to be considerate to the fact that we're a few years behind. I look up to my big sister completely, and I always have, and it's very easy to hurt my feelings when you're mean to me. {She gets all choked up. This is the first time anyone has ever shed an actual tear during one of my interviews.} Especially when you put me on the "Poopy" list, and on the "Pesky" list is your bowling team. {I'm sorry, Lizzie. I'll try from now on to be sweeter.}

What are the disadvantages of being the younger sister?

Your parents see big sister's mistakes, so little sister is supposed to come out perfect, and no matter what, you're always the baby, and being a baby entails always having to know that your opinion isn't always the important one.

What has growing up with an older sibling taught you about life ?

Appreciate your sister when you live with her, 'cuz when you move away you'll miss her.

If you have siblings, write their names down here: _____

_____

In what ways are you similar?

_____

_____

_____

_____

_____

_____

_____

In what ways are you different?

_____

_____

_____

_____

_____

_____

_____

Script Yourself

Have you ever been watching a movie and been so distracted by how lame a character sounds that you missed the plot completely? Or have you ever seen a sitcom with a good story premise, but thought you could've written one much funnier? Well, without the right script, your movie or show is guaranteed to be a bomb. Think of your fave film . . . Chances are more than likely that the lead characters were portrayed as intelligent folks who always said the right, moving thing to make your mascara runny from crying *Pretty in Pink* (boo-hoo) or *Sixteen Candles* (tee-hee) style tears. Don't we all wish the best Hollywood scriptwriter could dream up lovely things for us to say on a daily basis? And how cool would it be if you could expand your vocab a lil' so you could speak as eloquently as Princess Grace Kelly, or with a whiplash wit as quick as Mae West, and give spicy comebacks as icy as Bette Davis? Well, it may sound *impossible*, but in the Pesky dictionary *that* word is never featured.

You and I are now going to rewrite your script to make you act like YOU are the sharpest pencil wearing lipstick. After all, you are Pesky, and a Pesky girl knows how to be outspoken but never rude . . . and how to be bitingly clever without being crude. The purpose of any dialogue in a flick is to tell a memorable story, one that will touch another person's heart. Our goal when using the gift of speech should be to make friends and other listeners into fans, by creating an unforgettable story that will inspire. I will now give you all the awesome tips I have acquired in learning to be a righteous outspoken babe . . . with no fear of what anyone else thinks of my philosophies on life, or the crazy made-up words I love to include in my vocab. Future big-mouthed & beautiful speech-givers of the world unite! Let's scream our pink poetry loud and clear!

Characters whose speaking style I'd love to emulate:

Liza Minnelli as Sally Bowles in *Cabaret*, because she's so original . . . especially when she describes her green nail polish as being "divinely decadent". . . which is something I'd never heard a person say without making it sound completely snobby. And she's blatantly honest without ever sounding crass. Any character from those superclassy & highly snazzy 1930s screwball comedies . . . the kind where all the women possessed whiplash wit, spoke really fast, and *always* had the last word. Rosalind Russell personified this era as the only woman reporter on a big-city newspaper in *His Girl Friday*. Barbara Stanwyck in *The Lady Eve* is another ingenious character who is so sharp that she makes all the boys look like himbos . . . without ever dropping an uncouth curse word from her lips. I always try to model my speaking style after this kind of old-fashioned elegance. It makes me feel fancy, and boys find it mucho alluring as well.

Describe a film character whose speaking style you admire:

_____

_____

_____

ANOTHER PESKY POINT—Try to pay attention to how your demeanor and speech patterns differ around different groups of people. Are you extra shy around cutie patootie boys? Do you curse like a truck driver around your girlfriends? Are you a brat from hell around the parents? A certain amount of multicharacter development is swell, just as long as you're not pulling a lil' Miss Jekyll & Hyde routine. I mean, you wouldn't want to walk up to grandma and say, "What up, bee-atch?" . . . so think about your audience before experimenting with new speaking styles, because to certain people it might sound lame, or just inappropriate. Eventually, you'll map out a recognizable character you will portray. It takes years of soul searching to figure out what kind of girl you want to emulate, but it is something to think about, and in the end it's a lot less work than having to play all those different roles around all those various folks. There are some scripts that should never make it to the big screen, so . . .

Welcome to the Cutting Room Floor

This is where we will edit out all the "garbage" from your otherwise purrfect vocabulary, and get you truckin' down that road to sounding like a "reel" queen of the silver screen.

A deadly case of the "likes"—This is the numero uno sin of all teen talk! Can I tell you this, "like," story, okay? I grew up in the San Fernando Valley in the '80s. My fave band was the GoGo's, and I practically lived at the Sherman Oaks Galleria, which was the setting for such flicks as *Fast Times at Ridgemont High* and *Valley Girl*. I grew up in a time and place where learning when and where to insert the holy word *like* was treated as an art form. In my hood, you were considered a leper if you were sans "likes." When I hit eighteen I wanted to be taken seriously as an adult, but "Are you, like, hiring like right now?" is not the least bit professional. I was starting to despise my acquired "like"-ness. This is how I was saved: Before actually saying a thought out loud, I would think it through in my mind and make sure it was exactly what I wanted to say, minus any "likes." This process sounds lengthy, but in actuality it only takes as much as a slight pause in conversation. I also found that taking this pause has improved my speech pattern all around. It has given me that extra second to rethink potentially hurtful or offensive comments and gives me time to choose my words creatively. This tiny pause will make you sound even smarter, more confident, and it will help to get rid of your little L-word problem once and for all!

Ya know ? ? ?—Do you want to give every person you speak to the impression that you are on a mad search for their approval? If the answer is no, then I would suggest editing "you know?" from the end of your sentences. I too am guilty of this, and to fix it I will use the same method applied in removing the "likes" from my life's script. Let's conquer this together . . . you know?

"Funner" and "It was so fun"—These are small but deadly annoyances. First of all, "funner" is not a word, and nothing can be "so fun" . . . it's missing an adverb. The proper way to convey this state of bliss is to say that you had "so MUCH fun" . . . voilà!

Me, myself, and I—Instead of saying "Me and my mom went to Bloomie's," you should give "my mom and I" a try, dahhling! Doesn't it sound all the more dazzling? Let's try it once more, shall we? "Me and Randolph rented *Bride of Chucky* last night." . . . Sounds distasteful, yes? How 'bout this . . . "Randolph and I rented *Lolita* last night." Trés classy!

The final Script Edit:

All you need to do in order to sound purrfectly pleasing is simply listen to yourself. What you say can reveal a lot about how truly confident you feel, so in order to come across as a self-esteem guru, you must first veto the following ultra-nasty habits . . .

CURSIN', SWEARIN', TALKIN' SH*T—Saying crude things is sooo passé, not to mention that it's what adults expect you to do, so that makes you something truly lame . . . predictable! Most adults, bosses, and parents are banking on you being irresponsible and not too bright, due to your lack of life experience. Well, there's one way to shock the pants off the 'rents at this point, and that would be to all of a sudden sound like a Harvard-educated socialite! It's not hard, all it takes is a lil' concentration.

Here's a prime example (à la cinema réalité) . . . There once was this kooky purple Mohawked punker girl who was interning after school at a record label. Let's call her "Jennifur" . . . anyway, bunches of cuties and "suits" dismissed her at first based on how she looked (a lot of the dismissing may have had to do with the silver chain running from her nostril to her third ear pierce). However, once the conserv' staff actually spoke to the odd-looking girl, the dismissing went missing! They realized that "Jennifur" was just as smart as any of them, and were impressed by how she favored old-fashioned sayings instead of cursing. Out of her black-lip-lined mouth came sweet advice, extensive knowledge of classic films and rock music, and manners rivaling a real princess, Grace Kelly. The staff came to respect her despite her freaky looks, and even threw her a going-away party when she decided to quit (with proper notice, of course!). I think being so well spoken pleasantly shocked them more than any daring–do could have offended them.

you owe it to your audience!

Here is some swanky 1940s-type lingo you can use instead of the usual 4-letter word:

Holy (INSERT WORD HERE)! . . . In place of the overused phrase "Holy sh*t!" why not try using nice creative words that will entertain your listener as well? I love saying things like "Holy eyelashes!" "Holy Apple Jacks!" or even "Holy kitty cats!"

As for the F word . . . please say anything BUT! Just eliminate it, and use fanciful phrases in its place. Instead of saying you've been "f*#?d over" . . . why not say that you've been "horn swoggled," like the old movie cowboys used to.

Instead of calling bad girls "sluts" or something equally vulgar . . . Call them "vixens" or "harlots." These words aren't as critical (and even sound kinda cool), but you end up sounding more self-confident when you're not putting down other girls.

Am I "on the level"? This one is my fave, and I got it from watching tons of Jean Harlow and 40s crime flicks. It was the cool people's way of asking if you are telling the truth. So instead of "no sh*t?" . . . how 'bout "are you on the level?". "Strictly on the level" can also be used to start a story that sounds too crazy to be true . . . It's simply so hep, cats!

Your next shindig isn't a Par-tay . . . it's a "soiree"! Doesn't that sound très fanc-ay?

"Oh, brother!" . . . is a great response to anything shocking that happens. As a fab substitute for the all too common phrase "Oh, sh*t," it gives what your saying more impact. Try saying it out loud . . . "Ohhh, brrr-uther!" . . . See? Or you can always use sultry star Greta Garbo's fave substitute: "Oh applesauce!"

"Say . . . What gives?" . . . is another phrase I've heard used a lot on the American Movie Classics channel. It's good for when you catch your mom looking through your drawers, or a classmate peeking at your test answers, or your friend makes a weird comment about you that you'd like explained further.

Remember . . . when you have the urge to use an uncouth word, only one extra second of thought is all it takes to think of something more creative to put in its place. I mean, when you think of Elizabeth Taylor, do you picture her running around town saying "Fu*k you!" and "You A$$hole"? Or do you picture her being too princesslike for those kind of immature linguistics? Well, so are you, dahhling . . . so give yourself a lingo makeover à la Audrey Hepburn in *My Fair Lady*, and pretty soon your whole school will be following in your eloquently platformed footsteps.

Putting yourself down—You know the score . . . "I'm fat," "I'm ugly," "I suck at this" . . . these kind of negative statements only make things seem a lot worse than they really are, not to mention that your friends constantly have to disagree, which is really tiresome for them. Instead of dwelling on the things you think you "suck at," or the weight you want to lose, try thinking about the things you know you rock at, and make a conscious effort to have a funky fab time doing anything and everything . . . even if you DO suck at it. The fastest way to feel cruddy, and lose friends simultaneously, is to drain everyone's happy energy by complaining about superficial issues. So make sure you leave those self-deprecating thoughts behind you as you walk out your bedroom door every morning, and concentrate on having the rockin' fun time you so much deserve.

Wanna wanna wanna—The "I wanna" girls bug the Pucci pants off me . . . "I wanna design clothes," "I wanna learn to play guitar," "I wanna start my own 'zine." . . . it's so annoying to hang out with people who say this every three seconds yet never seem to actually DO anything about it! They are also known as the "One day I'll . . ." gals. Don't waste all your creative energy blabbing about things you're "gonna" do . . . just get started on achieving your dreams now, and shush up about it. Don't make me use the Nike motto!

Not accepting compliments—When someone says something flattering to you, say THANK YOU! People usually think about a compliment before bestowing it upon you (and it takes a lil' bit of guts), so the most ungracious thing for you to do is to downplay it by saying "No, i'm not!" or making a sarcastic joke. This puts the other person on the spot and makes them feel rejected. Smart girls relish in positive comments from others'. I like to think of sweet flattery as an invisible good-luck charm hanging around my neck for the rest of the day. Sweet compliments are to be collected in our consciousness, not tossed away carelessly.

"Only boring people get bored"—These are brilliant words of wisdom brought to you by Mom. I live by these words . . . not to sound too ultra-perky, but life is such a awesome concept! How could you ever be bored? Uttering these painful words "i'm bored" . . . seems so ungrateful and makes you look like an uncreative person. If you are so bored, then find something entertaining to do . . . carry a book in your purse, sketch people, invent Pesky games, try to have a party in your own head—and before you know it, others will be partying along with you, and "bored" will be banished from your life . . . *and* vocab.

> "The sweetest kittens have the sharpest claws."
> —Russ Meyer

"BACKSTAGE WHISPERS"

Becoming a gauche & gossiping Gertie—Telling lots of lil' white lies and gossiping *will* get you into trouble. Why don't you leave the high drama and backstabbing to Will Shakespeare and Bette Davis. Spreading rumors will in the end only get YOU some bad reviews as a person not to be trusted.

Freaks and geeks—Making fun of other kids at school is ultra-lame, and makes you look like you have nothing better to do than hurt the feelings of innocent nerds. I do not care if it is the class "pizza face," the "scary death-rock girl," or the future computer programmer . . . please put the kibosh on insulting anyone else in the future . . . and maybe then you can start to regain some good karma, so you don't end up as the butt of someone else's insults later in life. If you spread warmth and kindness, you can be sure that life will lead you on a glammy path, instead of a cruddy ol' dirt road. Abide by the belief of the white witches (I learned this from that movie *The Craft*): Whatever you put out there comes back three times stronger . . . so when having the urge to join in a game of torture the freak, let that piece of wisdom staple your mean trap shut.

Hold that thought . . . Interrupting is one of the rudest things you can do to someone during a conversation, so try to be concious of it if you are known as an interrupter. Make sure you let people finish their train of thought, even if what they are saying is dullsville . . . but if their train of thought is chugging by for more than ten minutes, and there is no caboose in sight, then by all means say something! It is also okay to cut someone off verbally if they are telling you something that is going down the wrong track. Say something direct, yet not rude, like "That's a little more information than I needed," "Don't go there!," or in a dire conversational emergency try "Hold that thought . . . I really need to go powder my nose!"

Conversation

List all of the un-Pesky words you would like to edit from your otherwise purrfect script:

_____   _____

_____   _____

_____   _____

_____   _____

_____   _____

_____   _____

drawings by Jennifer

PERFORMANCE ANXIETY!

Spotlight on: The Shy Pesky Girl . . . the one who has all these fab creative opinions and groovy ideas in her lovely head. Yeah . . . I'm talking to you . . . Do you ever feel like you know exactly how you want to sound but are too intimidated to actually blurt out what you're thinking? I was at one time a shy wallflower of a girl, and it had nothing to do with yummy Jakob Dylan either. It was just about insecurity. I knew deep inside that I possessed an outspoken Pesky Meddling soul, but finding the golden key to unlock it was a big artistic process. It was as if I had to go through a labyrinth before speaking, while others just opened their mouths and out it came! I became a silent movie star in front of my Hollyweird hipster friends . . . thinking it was better to say nothing than risk seeming nerdy. One day . . . I had a revelation while watching these same hipsters throw chairs at one another on Jerry Springer . . . REALLY! I watched for a moment, then realized . . . I always had much more to say than these clowns, and here they were on TV! I could definitely handle speaking in front of my tiny viewing public. I vowed to be mute no more!

One way I conquered my introverted tendencies was to get reacquainted with my inner preschooler! If you recall, in preschool we were not afraid to speak our minds. We were brand-spankin'-new people, so we had no time to develop weird inhibitions and awkwardness (those joys were saved for the teen years) . . . to play was the thing! My motto . . . "I am the boss of my own self," which must have been the psychic precursor to my Pesky mantra, "Life is a movie starring you!" In preschool, the "boss" statement was effective . . . no other kids even tried to give me orders! I still chant this in my mind when I am feeling shy or intimidated. Try to go back to the swing-set era in your mind . . . and remember that you *are* the boss of your own self . . . and this is *your* movie!

ekp

PESKY THINGS TO DO:

★ Practice introducing yourself to new people whenever possible. (Remember to give firm handshakes and always say "nice meeting you" before walking away)

★ Try to make lots of eye contact when speaking to anyone. (This is a great tool in helping you to look confident.)

★ Read a new book, or see the newest flick, so you'll always have an interesting topic of conversation to spout out.

★ Remember that everyone is shy in some way. If nobody initiated conversation with anybody else, then we'd all be talking to ourselves . . .

Write here the things you've regretted saying out loud:

_____

_____

_____

Write down something you've regretted *not* saying out loud:

_____

_____

_____

P.esky **S**.ecret: It's better to regret something nerdy that you did say than to regret something brilliant that you didn't!

What was your most embarrassing moment?

_____

_____

_____

_____

_____

And when you've deposited that painful moment here, you no longer have to mentally carry it around . . . you can just revisit it on this page when you feel the need.

Revenge of the Nerds—Attention all nerdettes . . . raise your hands! A great creative writing teacher once told me that the only students who wind up really looking stupid are the ones who think they are too cool to ask questions in class! No question is too lame if you honestly don't know the answer. Once you get the answers to your inquiries . . . you aquire knowledge, and KNOWLEDGE, my little kittens, is PESKY POWER. So get those nerdy little hands in the air and wave them like you just don't care . . . Vive le pocket protector revolution!

Who do you find to be an absolute genius?

_____
_____
_____
_____
_____

What makes you cry tears of joy?

_____
_____
_____

What makes you cry sad tears?

_____
_____
_____

LUNCH

FILM HISTORY

FRENCH LIT

ORGANIC CHEM

Lizzie's Inspirational Motto :
"What makes me a freak only makes me more beautiful, so live with it!"

Now here comes the ultra-thrilling part of our glammy vocab makeover section . . . the Pesky things you SHOULD write into your star-studded script . . .

GEEK CHIC—Expand your vocab nerd style! First, start by looking up any word you don't understand in a lil' pocket dictionary. Next, use your fave color marker or fun glitter stickers, to mark each word you've looked up. I adore flipping through my *Webster's* to view the impressive amount of new vocab I've collected.

CREATING YOUR OWN ADJECTIVES IS A CREATIVE THANG TO DO, NOT TO MENTION Glittertastically Rockin'licious!—Add some Pesky razzle-dazzle to your va-va-vocab. SOME NOT so official words I dig using are; glammy, Pesky-fied, purr-fect, de-voom . . . you can also turn anything into an adjective by adding *esque* on the end: "Your new red 'do is so Ringwald-esque!" It doesn't matter how absurd your words sound . . . I'd bet my vintage Pucci purse that your friends will be biting off your lingo within 24 hours.

Fantabulous!

POSITIVELY PESKY—The next time someone bags on you, Think Pink instead of seeing red! Never carry other people's negative baggage around, save up for a set of Louis Vuitton instead. Why not try feeling sorry for your harsh critics, instead of eye-lashing out. I would not have survived high school, if I hadn't realized that my cruelest critics were having an even worse teen-time than I was.

TRICK OR TREAT—Hand out compliments as if they were Hershey's Kisses on Halloween! Making someone else feel glam is a groovy thing to do. You should always acknowledge the rockin' success of others' accomplishments and be genuinely happy for a friend trying to live out her dreams. Then, when it's your turn to hitch a ride on that same meteoric fame star, she'll be there to sprinkle *you* with mental confetti.

TESTING 1-2-3—So, you want people to really hear what you have to say? Then there's just one thing you need to do: Listen! All great actresses know this secret, and it is their key to success. You can't create a rewarding dialog with anyone if you're always worried about what *you* are going to say next, and not paying attention to what is being said to you. One of the highest compliments you can receive is "She's a swell listener!" It makes you seem like a smart pink iMac computer that is busy gathering entertaining data. So, the next time you are at a Pesky-style soiree . . . stop, look, and listen !

Remember that the most important thing you can bring to any social event is not what you wore, how much booze you brought, or if you had the hottest date . . . it's always what you said. The words you leave behind make the most lasting impression, so make them intelligent, polite, and Pesky of course.

What are some of your fave words?

_____

_____

_____

_____

_____

_____

_____

Start collecting some of your own purrsonal lingo here:

_____

_____

_____

_____

PESKY THINGS TO DO:

Carry a journal or tiny scrapbook around with you at all times. It will give you a place to write all your secret thoughts, glue souvenirs from every place you visit . . . not to mention it looks all hipster & beatniky to whip one out. People will whisper, "Who's the profoundly cool poetess over there?"

Read fairy tales.

Collage your school notebook.

 Read autobios & bios of inspirational women who've changed herstory. After all, there are many fascinatin' subjects to choose from . . . Jackie O., Marie Antionette, Edith Head, Josephine Baker, Mae West, Evita, Anne Frank, Jacqueline Susann, Marianne Faithfull, Dorothy Parker, Oprah, Greta Garbo, Maria Callas, Yoko Ono, Mary Pickford, Lucille Ball, Tina Turner, Elizabeth Taylor, Carmen miranda, Madonna, and oh so many more! Try to read at least one a month.

Remember: Every word that escapes those Revlon red lips should be a purrfect tribute to the classy, Pesky star that you are . . . featuring Oscar speech worthy syllables of insight . . . all creating a unique life story that will make everyone stop, look, and listen.

ekp

"The best fashion accessory is a good book . . . and high-heeled shoes . . . I like them as well."
—designer Vivienne Westwood

Research for a Great Script

Here are some of my fave inspirational Pesky books to help you with your script:

Tall Tales by **Jerry Hall**—You know her as Mrs. Mick Jagger, but to me she's as iconic as Marilyn or Mae West . . . and that's some high-falutin praise coming from moi! When I was only a lil' whippersnapper, I used to cherish sneaky peeks at my mom's haughty *Cosmo* mags, and Jerry was always my fave cover goddess. I later spotted her on the cover of Roxy Music's glam-rock album, *Siren,* dressed as a glittery buxom blue mermaid. Not only is she the woman I'd most love to look like, but she is brilliant as well! Her pals have included such luminaries as Salvador Dalí and Andy Warhol. She wrote this book in '85, and it's my inspirational bible . . . I carry it around in my purse and read quotes from it when I'm in the need for some insta-glam. Jerry grew-up in a trailer park, and when she was eighteen, her mom saved up to buy Jerry a one-way ticket to Paris so she could follow her dream of becoming a star. Armed with only a Frederick's of Hollywood gown, and a string bikini, she made her fantasies come true! She gave me hope that a girl like me can be noticed using Pesky purrsonality, and by standing tall on her own two marabou mules. Hall's a doll!

Edith Head's Hollywood—A must for any aspiring fashion designer . . . Edith was the most legendary of all movie wardrobe mistresses. She was at one time even more famous than the celebs she dressed. In fact, her office became a star attraction on the Universal Studios Tour in the '70s. Some of the girls she so breathtakingly dolled up were . . . Grace Kelly, Liz Taylor, Audrey Hepburn, Sophia Loren, Mae West, Bette Davis, and Natalie Wood . . . to name only a fraction of her sparkly client list.

A Girl Like I—An enchanting autobio of Hollywood's first—and most talented—girl screenwriters . . . **Anita Loos.** This book takes place in my fave era . . . the roaring '20s, and it's written with such savoir faire! As a teen she penned a short book as a joke to one of her boyfriends, called *Gentlemen Prefer Blondes.* The joke was on this lil' brownette 'cuz she became a superstar overnight! She went from living in a tent on the beach . . . to having tea with Mussolini at The Ritz in Paris! Her mantra was so Pesky . . . "Never be bored."

Any book about **Marilyn Monroe**—She's history's most vulnerable, inimitable, irreplacable angel of glamour. In a sea of Oscar-winners, nobody shined as brightly as her. mmmm ♥ ♥ *it's marilyn!*

Marilyn Monroe courtesy of Bernard of Hollywood™

Any book about **Jayne Mansfield**—Star of *The Girl Can't Help It* . . . Jayne was a va-va-voom blonde, lived in a Beverly Hills mansion dubbed The Pink Palace, which was fully equipped with a heart-shaped swimming pool, would take her pet leopard for daily walks down Hollywood Blvd., drove the only pink Cadillac in L.A., while housing an impressive IQ of 163 in her seemingly bubbly beehive. Now that's what I call Pesky. Jayne is, to put it in her words . . . "Simply de-voom!"

D.V. by **Diana Vreeland**—She was editrix-in-chief for both *Harper's Bazaar* and *Vogue*, in the '40s to the '70s, where she reigned like a scarlet empress in her leopard print & hell-red office. Cool facts about D.V.: Her suits were tailored by Coco Chanel herself, unbeknownst to most she was Jackie Kennedy's purrsonal style advisor, she founded the costume department at the Metropolitan Museum of Art, and was first to hire Twiggy and Cher as models when the other editors thought them to be freaks. I could go on for ages, dahhling! If I was stranded on a planet in outer space and could have only one book to keep me company, this would be it . . . red-manicured hands down!

"We all need a splash of bad taste . . . NO taste is what I'm against. "—DIANA VREELAND

Weetzie Bat by **Francesca Lia Block**—This book is so "us" that it should be re-titled *Weetzie, The Pesky Meddling Girl*. She's a strong, creative, and whimsical role model, who's school attire includes palm tree sunglasses and an Indian feather headdress. I wish she really exisited so we could be best furrends. I became so obsessed with this book that I begged the author to come with me for hot chocolate, and she signed my book "To Jennifur, who is verrry Weetzie." Could you just die? It's a punk-rock-fairy-tale about a soul–searching girl living in Hollyweird, who encounters a genie that grants her three wishes. I won't give anything away, but to quote Weetzie . . . it's "slinkster cool."

P.esky **S.**ecret: Some of these books are out of print, so you may have to scour through dusty used-book shops in order to find them. Digging through the literary graveyards is another one of my most beloved hobbies. But if you are not a hard–core scavenger like I . . . then there's always this crazy magical thing called "the Internet" for you to explore. Happy hunting!

What books would you recommend I read?

_____

_____

_____

_____

_____

Stage Presence...
When You Get Some, It's Simply De-voom!

PMGs thrive on attention. People are always asking me, "Jennifur, why does everybody always pay the most attention to you?" It's because I've taught myself to just naturally demand attention when I walk into a room. I concentrate on emitting STAR QUALITY (okay, my own vintagey-Pesky-geeky form of stardom) . . . us girls won't be ignored, and the only way to receive recognition is to deserve recognition. It's a glowing attitude that comes from within, but must not be mistaken for a snobby or—how shall I say this politely? I can't—bitchy attitude (both of which are so very un-Pesky). It's sweet 'tude- but not saccharine. It is in the way you enunciate when you speak so every word you say sounds melodic, or in the way you stand up straight with your unique head held up high. You can carry an air about you that says "I'm talented and very intriguing, so you should praise me at least slightly."

Pesky thang to keep in mind—To recieve attention, you must pay attention. People who actually are interested in those around them will reap the rewards of others' attention. It's the Pesky golden-glitter rule!

Action!

It's a... Pesky Paper Doll!

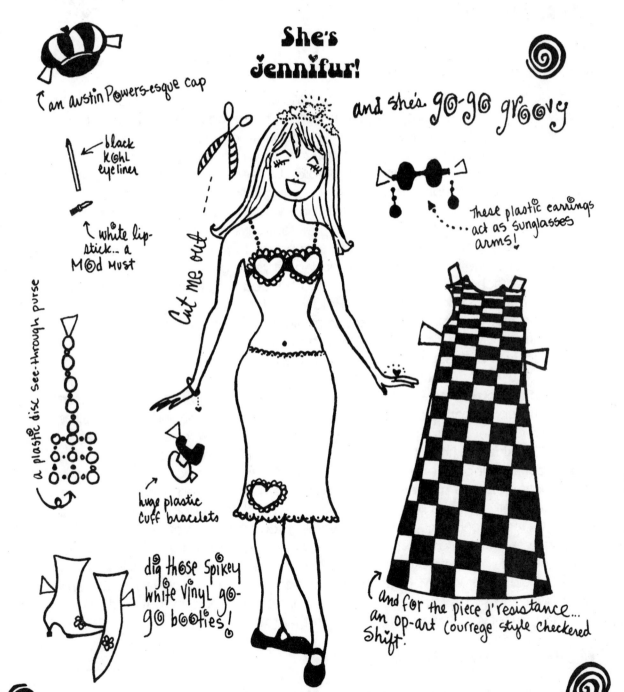

She's Jennifur!

and she's go-go groovy

↑ an austin Powers-esque cap

← black kohl eyeliner

↑ white lipstick... a Mod Must

these plastic earrings act as sunglasses arms!

a plastic disc see-through purse

Cut me out

huge plastic cuff bracelets

dig these spikey white vinyl go-go booties!

↑ and for the piece d'resistance... an op-art courrege style checkered shift.

She's going dancing at The Factory with Andy Warhol circa 1967.

artwork by yours truly :)

Putting On a Pesky Production

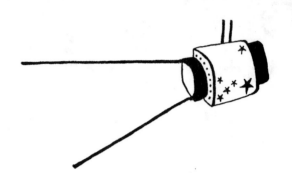

"What do you want to be when you grow up?" used to be a question commonly asked of teens, but the reason our generation rocks is because it's no longer about what you're going to be in the future . . . it's about what you're going to be NOW. Why wait to fulfill your dreams? Why not start to work on achieving your goals today? It is now more common than ever before for teens to become full-fledged entrepreneurs, and it's easier than you think. Starting a tiny business for yourself rocks. It teaches you how to discipline yourself, and you end up being strict, because there is no boss to whine to or feed excuses to, it's just you out there, baby! And don't think pure luck will bring imminent success; in fact, I find it rather annoying when people say to me, "You got a book deal at your age? You are just so lucky!," like some leprechaun fell out of the sky and handed it all to me free of charge. Luck's got nothing to do with it, honey. Hard work, dedication and research do. I've spent every day for the last nine years of my teen life promoting my Pesky Empire and getting my voice heard. If you win the lottery, okay . . . that's lucky, but it doesn't apply in business situations, where your success lies in your performance. It all trains you for adult life. For instance . . . I was terrible on the phone with professional people before I started doing my 'zine. But once I made myself start calling publicity departments of record labels for CDs to review, and movie studios for passes to review flicks, I practiced so much, that I am now a telephone wiz . . . no more shaking as I hold a receiver, or stuttering as I pretend to sound "mature." I figured out that nobody expects me to be an adult when I'm not, and a lot of the folks I spoke to said I was a breath of fresh air every time I called because I was so kooky and worked words like "glammy" or "de-voom" into our conversation, and called the receptionists "kitty cat." Another thing you can do is start doing research. Learn all you can by asking tons of Pesky questions, and reading trade papers about the field you're interested in . . . just like anyone who wants to be a Hollywood player would read *Variety*, and aspiring fashion designers would read *Women's Wear Daily*. The more you know, the more impressed people in that field will be when they meet you. Be yourself, and the rest will follow.

Who do you most want to grow up to be like? _____

_____

_____

What is your current passion in life? Brainstorm alone or with friends about how you could come up with a business plan, and raise some money to start a lil' biz. (Parents are a good bet in this arena, you most probably will have to seem dedicated, organized, and serious if they are going to front you any dough, though.) In case you are at a loss for happenin' ideas, I'll throw some your way, and perhaps one will spark a dazzling idea . . .

Be a fashion designer! Customize vintage clothes by either covering artsy tee-shirts with puffy paint or buying cheap vintage clothes and adorning them in rhinestones with a Bedazzler.

Manage your friends' band by introducing yourself to club & coffee house bookers.

Offer to walk your neighbors' dogs or to feed their pets while they're out.

Start a baby-sitters' club. (I know it's cliché, but it rakes in the moolah.)

Do a fanzine! Your school actually sets aside a mandatory hour every day for you to work on your 'zine . . . it's called "math class".

 Choreograph a crazy routine with some friends and entertain at kid's birthday parties.

REMEMBER! Just be patient and hang in there. Your empire can't be built in a week. It takes a little time and commitment.

List all the jobs you've had: _____

_____

What creative projects do you dream about taking on? (Hey!...What's stopping you?)

_____

_____

_____

Of which accomplishment are you most proud? _____

_____

_____

 "Do something you LOVE doing, and no matter what, you'll be able to sell it."
—pop artist ANDY WARHOL

PESKY THINGS TO DO:

 Practice the three R's of design . . . Research, Rip out, and Rework. Without my books, old magazines, scrapbooks, scissors, and glue . . . I would never find peace within myself. Collaging and creating things is so therapeutic. It makes me feel all zen and calm. It's my purrsonal form of meditation.

 Volunteer time (or donations) to help fight for a cause you believe in. I know this is going to sound all cheesified, but it's true . . . We are the future! We need to be proactive. Some organizations I support are People for the Ethical Treatment of Animals, breast cancer research, and anything to help the environment. It not only makes this world a groovier place to play in, but it makes you feel so proud of yourself.

If an advertisement, or something you see on TV offends you, write a letter to the company telling them why. All the major corporations DO pay close attention to all the complaints they get, so lil' ol' you *can* make a difference.

List all the ways in which you are making this a Pesky-er planet to live on:
(like planting flowers, not littering, getting your pets fixed, recycling, etc .):

_____

_____

"Imagination is more important than knowledge"—Albert Einstein

Write down a quote that inspires you most at the moment:

_____

You have been crowned Pesky Princess of your Queendom. What laws do you create?

_____

_____

SOME OF THE THINGS I COLLECT ARE . . .
wooden box purses from the '60s, Twiggy memorabilia, '70s Vogue mags, fashion books, records, vintage gowns, original posters from my fave flicks, Peter Max stuff, crazy pink hats, and cute boys.

List all the things you collect:_____

_____

_____

_____

Pesky

We can be whatever we wish to become, live out our dreams, create a whole new environment in which to live. I have a very purrsonal story to tell you . . . About when I first discovered my destiny . . . my dream, and my future. It was in the tenth grade, and a friend who worked at a magazine that reviewed punk music gave me a gift he thought I would have fun reading. It was a garbage bag filled with teens' homemade fanzines from around the U.S. I stayed up all night reading these badly Xeroxed pamphlets covering everything from film reviews to shocking purrsonal stories of relationships gone wrong. I was simply awestruck. It was as if the holy goddess of fanzines has sent me a sign in a Hefty bag from the artistic heavens via my friend Cake (yes, that's his name) as to what I was supposed to do with my life. I honestly believe that pile of rants and raves was my first true love. It was the first thing that looked easy to me. I tried tons of other things that i had hoped would fulfill my need for a purpose . . . guitar lessons (messed up my manicure), record company intern (too corporate), receptionist for the producer of the Emmys (he was such a slimy b✳st✳rd, I ran out sobbing one day never to return, and vowed never to watch that awards show unless I'm nominated), not to mention about twenty other flunked attempts at a career.

What I knew I did rock at was writing. I found my passion, and passion is what counts. The Hefty bag of 'zines was like a neon sign saying "Here is your chance to work at something you love, and you'll be the head honcho to boot!" What could be more purrfect? By the way, I'm not saying that your future lies in 'zinedom, just that you will find that neon sign flashing clues to what your future holds too. Just stay open-minded and be patient.

I bought a box of glue sticks and got busy. I broke all the rules of 'zine making. Most 'zines were all sloppily cut & pasted . . . whereas I wanted my 'zine to be pretty and girly. I took three days to collage each page (there went my social life) with lovely pictures of movie stars that I'd cut out of old magazines or Xeroxed out of my books on old Hollywood. Another thing that most 'zine-sters do is stick to one theme throughout an ish. My topics run the gamut from "The History of Heavy Metal" to "How to Dress Hep Like Katharine Hepburn." I wrote about everything I loved at that moment . . . my fave films, records, fashion tips, embarrassing stories, Hollywood gossip, interviews, all things girly . . . and boy-y too . . . like my purrsonal diary. I became the princess of my domain. It's healthy to know you rock no matter what anyone else says, and my 'zines allowed me to express myself on my own terms. Zoom in your Pesky pink hotrod to your final destination: Successville, Sweetie.

What do you know you are talented at? _____

_____

_____

List any contests, awards, and praises you've won: _____

_____

_____

When have you doubted yourself going into a situation,
and in the end were surprised with your own fabulocity? _____

_____

_____

What are your most cherished compliments? _____

_____

_____

What makes you blush? _____

_____

_____

"Love is all around, no need to waste it, you can have the town, why don't you
take it, you're gonna make it after all."—Theme from the Mary Tyler Moore show

LOOKS LIKE A GLITTERING FUTURE

Lizzie's movie is all about Photography. Here are her tips for taking the most rockin' photos:

Before I ever attended photography school, I was a picture-taking disaster! I once tried to take some nice portraits of my friend at the park, and after being developed, it looked more like a failed photo of a solar eclipse! Now that I have gone junior pro with my trusty camera, I am going to give you some advice I wish I'd gotten before wasting all that moolah at photo labs for full rolls of zip, zero, zilch . . .

 Give your model compliments and proper direction. Say things like "YES! that's purrrfect!" and "You look smashing, dahhling!"—very Austin Powers–like.

 Take photos of your best friends, or family members you have a real artistic connection to. It helps to feel 100% comfee around your model.

 Shoot for the stars! When you are taking a photo, try to channel the spirit of your fave star photographer, and it will bring you more confidence & style.

 Take risks, and be daring! Usually the most wacky, experimental shots you took as a joke process as the most visually stunning.

 Ask, ask, ask! Go to your local camera shop and ask tons of questions about film types, how to properly operate your camera for its best result, filters, lighting, anything you think of.

 Find a great local place to have your photos developed at a reasonable price. Most professional photo shops offer student discounts, so ask. *Good luck, my little shutterbugs!*

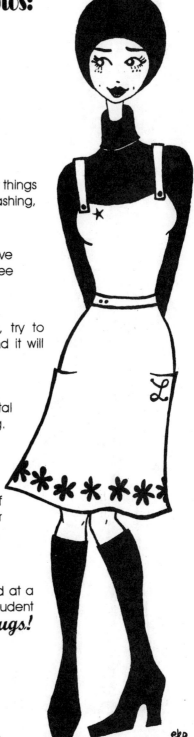

ekp

Here Are Some of My Fave Pesky Books on Fashion & Beauty

for the girl with a *Passion for Fashion*

THE POWER OF GLAMOUR: THE WOMEN WHO DEFINED THE MAGIC OF STARDOM by ANNETTE TAPERT—Whenever I'm at a loss for costume ideas, all I have to do is flip through this book, and voilà . . . Bombshell city! It pays homage to the flawless purrsonal style of the iconic 1930s silver screen goddesses . . . from Crawford to Garbo.

MAKING FACES by KEVYN AUCOIN—Step-by-step tips from my fave makeup artist on re-creating every look from '20s flapper to '70s disco dancer, and beyond! In this book he does elaborate makeovers on celebrity beauties, and creates personas for them to emulate . . . Tori Amos is The Innocent, Drew Barrymore is The Sophisticate, Courtney Love à la Jean Harlow is The Starlet, Julia Roberts looking very Rita Hayworth is The Siren, Lisa Marie Presley goes full-on Marilyn as The Bombshell, Winona Ryder, Janet Jackson, Gwyneth, Isabella, Kate Moss . . . the gang's all here, and they're de-gorgeous!

THE RUDI GERNREICH BOOK by PEGGY MOFFITT & WILLIAM CLAXTON—Rudi was the swinginest of all 1960s fashion designers, and Peggy Moffitt was his trippy MOD-el muse. This features hundreds of awe-inspiring photos of their fashion duets. Peggy wasn't merely a mannequin, she was more like a moving piece of op art, and she created eyeliner anarchy for girls everywhere!

FOUR FABULOUS FACES by LARRY CARR—Study through an archive of photos the magical mugs of Gloria Swanson, Marlene Dietrich, Greta Garbo, and Joan Crawford. My fave model Jerry Hall has said that she learned to pose by studying this book.

IN VOGUE: SIXTY YEARS OF CELEBRITIES AND FASHION FROM BRITISH VOGUE by GEORGINA HOWELL—If you'd like to get the entire lowdown on the history of fashion, then this is your textbook. Starting at the year 1916 (the true old skool) and ending in '75, this book is like a portable encyclopedia of all that is wearable and glam, and It's filled with thousands of exquisite photos for you to Xerox, and pin on your wall.

Glam Fact:

Did you know that the English word *glamour* was derived from the medieval word *gramarye*, which means "spell" or "witchcraft"? How wicked!

ekp

Welcome to . . .

The Wardrobe Department

Don't look unless you love daring Hollywood Fashions !

Welcome to . . .

The Wardrobe Department

Take This Test to See If You Have Pesky Style

Do you dig classic attire, with a dash of glitz & glam sprinkled on top?

Are you from the "something old, something new" school of dressing?

Do you take inspiration from the past?

Do you admire people who are "real" and live their lives to the fullest?

Do you dig putting your uniqueness on display?

Do old movies make you cry?

Are you excited about what the future holds?

Can you make every day into a party even when you're alone?

If you answered "YES" to these questions . . . then you are truly a Pesky girl, with Pesky purrsonal style as well. You are the future, and you're gonna help make it a much glammier time to live in. So . . .
ROCK ON, DOLL!

When I think about all my fave flicks, the costumes my fave screen goddesses wore are the very first thing that flashes through my mind in Technicolor. From Garbo's slouchy hats to Marilyn's infamous white dress to Alicia Silverstone's "very important" Alaïa dress in *Clueless* . . . We girls know that purrfecting our wardrobe is one of the most de-voomly important parts in making our Pesky movie come to life. The clothing we choose to adorn our bodacious bods is like a window into our artistic souls. So whilst inside that all-too-familiar whirligig of flying clothing (you know, the one that is formed in your mad rush to find the purrfect thing to wear) . . . I want you to take a deep yoga breath and think about the following . . . It's NEVER about how you look, it's all about how you FEEL.

One too many evenings I've left the house in an ensemble that may have made me visibly look skinnier, or sexier, but did not make me *feel* confident & comfee. Whenever I've gone out in an outfit I think I'm "supposed" to be wearing to "fit in," I always end up feeling insecure *and* out of place. Trying too hard will backfire, and you'll end up dreaming all night about your fave pair of Levi's waiting for you at home. On the other hand . . . there are those occasional evenings when you want to make a spectacle out of yourself. When you crave attention and want to give your crowd a show, GO FOR IT! As Hollywood costume design guru Edith Head once said . . . "You may not be able to change the size of your feet, or the shape of your legs, but you can always change the way you look."

If you feel 100% foxy in an ensemble, then grab your purse and go-go! But if you've slipped into something a lil' more uncomfortable to impress people, then do a strip routine, 'cuz, honey . . . you've got the wrong outfit on.

The trick is when getting dressed is to look in the mirror, and ask yourself one important question . . . "How do I feel?" or "Is life a movie starring moi in this ensemble?". Look deep into the catwalks of your soul, and envision your dream duds for the night. Then put on whatever is closest to your fantasy. If none of this works for you, then here's a tip . . . Levi's and a sparkly '50s sweater are always a hit.

If there's a flashy gown you're dying get for prom, and you're sure it makes you look va-va-voom, but your mom was thinking of something mint green that will ruin your life . . . then talk her through the sitch' like an adult. Here's a good place to start the conversation . . . "I always want to be honest with you, and I feel that the dress I've picked out will be appropriate for prom, because I'll feel pretty and confident in it, and I know it will make the evening that much more special if you'd let me get it" . . . and if she totally objects to your neon-pink tube gown with Velcro closures, then ask for her help in choosing a compromise. Parents will cut you more slack in wearing what you dig if you don't throw a diva fit about it . . . be polite about it. Learn this now and your college years will rock, but if your 'rents are hopelessly squaresville, and are preventing you from expressing yourself fully, then there are always large purses and Denny's bathrooms to assist you in a quick change.

Some Advice from My Pesky Mom...

My mom, being the style guru that she is, gave me some of the best advice a girl could use . . . She taught me that once you are out the front door, there is no turning back on what you have committed to wear. So you can forget about what you have on, hold your coiffed head up high, and trip the day fashion-tastic.

Budgeting Your Wardrobe

I bow to couture. I have been known on several occasions to weep while watching shows like *Fashion Television*. Pretty fabrics make my planet go round, but there's one problem with me housing this passion for fashion . . . I can't afford any of it. So instead, I have become expert at re-creating runway looks at thrift-shop prices. I am a deal doll, a bargain baby, a swap-meet sweetheart . . . The only essential, couturely speaking, is inspiration. It costs practically nothing to buy magazines about high fashion and create your own interpretation of the total look. We can all afford to be inspired by the gowns we see in *Vogue* . . . so don't feel sad that your allowance won't cover that new $10,000 psychedelic print Gucci dress . . . celebrate the fact that you can have the same look for only $10 at your local vintage shop, which is where Tom Ford of Gucci got the inspiration to do the dress in the first place. Girls who only buy head to toe designer looks are poseurs anyway. It's uncreative. Every outfit, even if it's Chanel, needs a little something strictly YOU sprinkled on top like fairy dust. The YOU touch makes it seem really original and innovative. Remember . . . great taste comes free of charge . . . and you've got it, baby doll!

Jennifur's Look

Today I'm going to call my visual statement "Glam-bohemian-hippie, Stevie Nicks, Marianne Faithfull, new wave milk-maid, 1923 meets 1973, Edwardian rock & roller chic!" Here's a list of the fashion items I'm currently worshiping:

* huge Bakelite bracelets
* rock band tees, customized by moi with rhinestones
* my hair's natural color (for the first time in ten years!)
* Frankenstein-esque platform boots
* Indian turquoise jewelry
* wearing the colors red & fuscia together
* Moroccan patchworked & mirrored fabrics
* Lenny Kravitz-inspired bell bottoms
* wearing tacky scarves as ascots
* Cher circa 1969
* New wave high-heeled booties in loud colors
* cloche hats from the 1920s (cloche means "bell" in French)
* anything with flared fairy sleeves or a handkerchief hem
* fitted '80s blazers covered in new wave band buttons
* a long black cashmere scarf stolen from my dad's closet (shhh!)
* original '70s vintage clothes by my fave designers (Ossie Clark, Vivienne Westwood, Yves St. Laurent, Chloe, Biba, Gunne Sax . . .)

She's groovy

★ ★ ★ ★ ★ ★ ★ ★ ★ ★ ★ ★ ★ ★ ★ ★ ★ ★ ★ ★

★ **Describe your current look:** ★ _____

_____

_____

_____

_____

_____

_____

_____

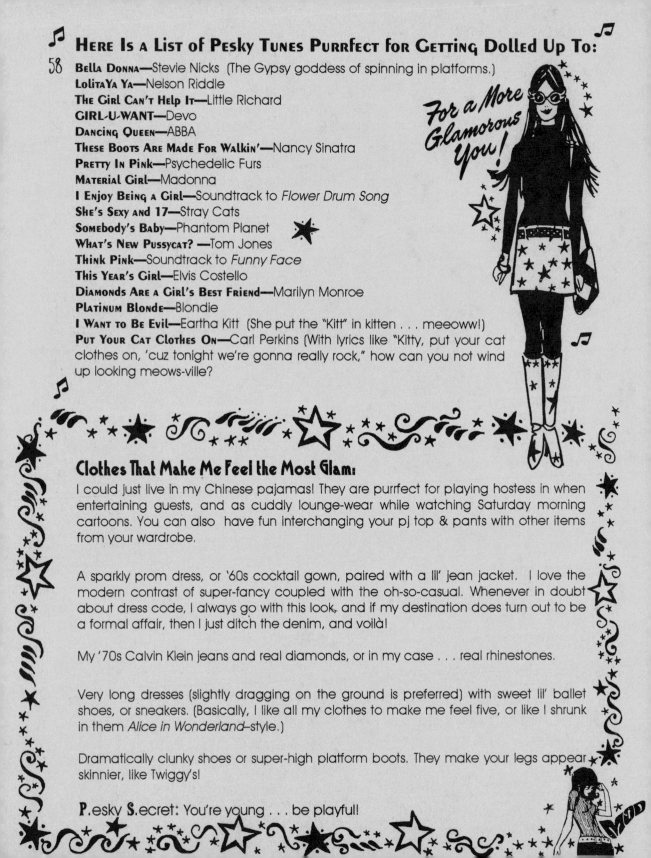

♪ Here Is a List of Pesky Tunes Purrfect for Getting Dolled Up To:

For a More Glamorous You!

- **Bella Donna**—Stevie Nicks (The Gypsy goddess of spinning in platforms.)
- **LolitaYa Ya**—Nelson Riddle
- **The Girl Can't Help It**—Little Richard
- **Girl-U-Want**—Devo
- **Dancing Queen**—ABBA
- **These Boots Are Made For Walkin'**—Nancy Sinatra
- **Pretty In Pink**—Psychedelic Furs
- **Material Girl**—Madonna
- **I Enjoy Being a Girl**—Soundtrack to *Flower Drum Song*
- **She's Sexy and 17**—Stray Cats
- **Somebody's Baby**—Phantom Planet
- **What's New Pussycat?**—Tom Jones
- **Think Pink**—Soundtrack to *Funny Face*
- **This Year's Girl**—Elvis Costello
- **Diamonds Are a Girl's Best Friend**—Marilyn Monroe
- **Platinum Blonde**—Blondie
- **I Want to Be Evil**—Eartha Kitt (She put the "Kitt" in kitten . . . meeoww!)
- **Put Your Cat Clothes On**—Carl Perkins (With lyrics like "Kitty, put your cat clothes on, 'cuz tonight we're gonna really rock," how can you not wind up looking meows-ville?

Clothes That Make Me Feel the Most Glam:

I could just live in my Chinese pajamas! They are purrfect for playing hostess in when entertaining guests, and as cuddly lounge-wear while watching Saturday morning cartoons. You can also have fun interchanging your pj top & pants with other items from your wardrobe.

A sparkly prom dress, or '60s cocktail gown, paired with a lil' jean jacket. I love the modern contrast of super-fancy coupled with the oh-so-casual. Whenever in doubt about dress code, I always go with this look, and if my destination does turn out to be a formal affair, then I just ditch the denim, and voilà!

My '70s Calvin Klein jeans and real diamonds, or in my case . . . real rhinestones.

Very long dresses (slightly dragging on the ground is preferred) with sweet lil' ballet shoes, or sneakers. (Basically, I like all my clothes to make me feel five, or like I shrunk in them *Alice in Wonderland*–style.)

Dramatically clunky shoes or super-high platform boots. They make your legs appear skinnier, like Twiggy's!

P.esky **S.**ecret: You're young . . . be playful!

Weight a Minute!

A message from your Pesky sponsor . . . On the subject of weight . . . Feeling depressed about your shape or size is not going to make you look any better, only acceptance will. Accept who you are, tell yourself all the complimentary things you need to hear in order to feel good about yourself. I know about this because I used to get really blue about my expanding tush. I'm voluptuous by nature, so I think to myself everyday . . . Mae West wouldn't have spent time doubting how wonderful each and every one of her curves were. And neither should you! Glam is something glittering that comes from the inside.

"A model's just an imitation of the real thing."—Mae West

List the things about your body that you know are totally cute:

_____

_____

PESKY THINGS TO DO:

Shop in the boys' dept. They seem to have fab basics you can never find in the girls' dept. In the little boys' dept. at Target, I found a pink button-down Oxford shirt, which totally looked like Ralph Lauren, adorable argyle socks, striped boxers to sleep in, and boot-cut Wrangler western jeans for like $12!

Throw away your scale! Judge your weight by how you *feel* about your bod, and how your fave slinky dresses fit.

A good thing about chubby legs . . .
Your knee socks stay up better.

List all the things you can remember dressing up as on Halloween: _____

_____

_____

What are you going to dress up as this Halloween? _____

_____

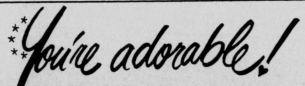

You're adorable!

VERY PESKY THINGS TO DO FOR YOUR WARDROBE

Go Monochrome-a-go-go—Dressing in one singular color from head to toe is the easiest way to flatter a figure, and look MOD-ly chic while doing so. Pick any color, but if you go with pink, or any other bright shade, make sure every item you're wearing is of the same exact hue, or you'll end up looking choppy. The most economical way to master this look is to pile on the noir. The color black has cast an eternal spell on fashion. It defies trends. It can convey a goth, futuristic, mod, arty, deco, or glam Hollywood vibe. Try a pair of ebony tights, black skirt or cigarette pants, noir turtleneck, any pair of jet shoes, and voilà! You are instantly streamlined, no matter what your weight.

I'm not saying black is the *only* color you should worship. We Pesky girls adore every color that makes us happy. I'm merely suggesting that cool gloomy night shade if you're in need of some unbiased suggestions from a new friend. Dressing monochromatically is such an effective way to look elongated, you'll never think "diet" again! Another tip: If your friends tire of seeing you in an all-black uniform, then just add one huge, brightly colored accessory to make an even more fun & fashion-y statement. How about a plastic cuff bracelet from the '80s? Day-Glo nail polish with glitter on top? Or go with a furry faux leopard coat . . . they look fantastique with every mono-color ensemb.

Mix pink with black or red—It's fun and totally '80s!

Don't fret if you have nothing new to wear. Remember that wearing an old dress which looks fabulous on your bod is much more effective than wearing a new dress that is only so-so on you—Some of the world's best-dressed women wear practically the same ensemb every day . . . Coco Chanel in her signature black suit, Tina Turner in micro-minis and stilettos, Katharine Hepburn in faded chinos and gardening togs, or Anna Sui in red lipstick & head-to-toe noir.

She's momochrome a-go-go! Her look was inspired by beatniky Audrey Hepburn in the film *Funny Face*

ekp

Read fashion magazines for inspiration, but never try to copy a look—Always come up with your own interpretation . . . A lot of women attempt to imitate the trendy designer look o' the moment, and all they end up looking like is just that . . . an imitation of the real thing.

If you haven't worn it in the past year . . . give it to someone who will—Neglected clothing is the result of buying an item of clothing, or a pair of shoes, that you simply "had to have", yet forgot to picture what you'd wear it with. When shopping, don't get carried away by these lovely yet hard to coordinate items. When you try something on, really try to envision how you'd wear it, and with what. I'm just the pot talking to all you kettles, because I'm totally guilty of this too. My weakness is black evening dresses on sale (Another Pesky rule: don't buy things just because they're cheap. If you'd never give it a second look at full price, pass it up on the sale rack!) I could attend a cocktail party every night for the next decade, but if you invite me to a barbeque game . . . I simply haven't got a thing to wear!

So, delve into your wardrobe and pull out anything you haven't worn in the past two years. Hold one item up at a time, and ask it the following questions . . . "Will I ever wear you?", "Are you worth the hard-earned cash I have to spend having you altered?" If the answers are NO, then bid them adieu. Give them to Goodwill, sell them at a resale shop, or have a clothes swapping party with your friends. Your mind—as well as your closet—will feel less cluttered.

Give your boring clothes a Pesky makeover—So there's this old pair of jeans living your closet that you've worn one too many times, to the point of mega-boredom! The solution? Give 'em some glam! Take the item over to your nearest fabric or hobby shop, and go wild! Should they display your fave band names in glitter puffy paint? Should you sew groovy '60s patches onto them? Or maybe they are crying out for some long fringe & glued-on feathers? Sew big sequins on them by hand . . . Be an artistic blue jean guru! If you are a wiz with a sewing machine, you could even turn them into a long denim skirt or Janis Joplin bell-bottoms, by cutting the seams and adding patchworked sections of bright fabrics to them. Plus . . . If you are sick of wearing the same jacket every day . . . then give it a new look too! cover it in new wave pins, or add a faux fur collar. You'll find by doing this that your wallet will be bursting, and so will your wardrobe.

Stay within your movie's budget—If your allowance won't cover the cost of a rhinestone tiara . . . then buy one of the glittery plastic ones that say Happy Birthday at your local party store. Not only are they cute—but you'll get a lot of attention, and if you're lucky . . . a free piece of cake.

"If in doubt overdress. If you look over-the-top you can make the most boring occasion have some interest. It's quite a generous thing to do."—designer **Vivienne Westwood**

Unless going for the Madonna's *Desperately Seeking Susan* look . . . keep your bra straps hidden, and that goes for unflattering panty lines too! Try to avoid the latter by investing in a great skin-toned torture-thong. Sometimes we must sacrifice comfort for beauty as ravishing as ours.

Treat your clothes like collectors' items—I do recommend saving up your dough to buy a super-ritzy thing at least once a year. Things like a plaid Burberry cashmere scarf or sweet Chanel ballet slippers . . . are called fashion investments . . . and if you take good care of them, they can make you a pretty bundle one day. The reason we all know these designers' names is because they are renowned for their craftsmanship and quality. If you buy five trendy $30 dresses that fall apart after one wash, then that would have been enough to buy those dreamed of Chanel shoes. Treating yourself to little symbols of status every blue moon is smart, and you deserve such luxuries. It's the same as collecting art, most of the high fashion stuff only grows in value long after the collections are gone from stores, even if they've been worn! All I'm saying is spend your money wisely . . . and even if you just can't afford the "big names," treat all your clothes as if they were Versaces: with lots of care, as well groomed as you are, cleaned, folded, hung up nicely on hangers, give them the works! After all, they are your Versaces.

Pesky stars who design and sew their own clothes . . . *If She Sews, She Knows*
Björk, Erykah Badu, Courtney Love, Shirley Manson, Melissa Auf Der Maur, Gwen Stefani

PESKY THING TO DO:

O Before exiting your boudoir, give yourself a quick glance in the mirror . . . Have doubts about anything? Or does something appear like it's trying too hard? Make sure you are always feeling like the confident bejeweled star you really are . . . with or without real diamonds.

O **Wear black . . . but THINK PINK!**

"Color makes a costume sing!"

Paste pics here of your dream outfits:

Rhinestones Are a Girl's Best Friend!

J'adore using the swanky word *accoutrement* . . . it's just a fancy word for "accessories"—à la Français. Knowing which jewels would properly accent your outfit is a total art form. If you purrfect the art of accessorizing, you become magician-like . . . knowing how to turn one dress . . . into twenty. It gives your ensemble a certain distinction, and the possibility of being utterly unforgettable. You just have to know what look you are trying to achieve. For instance, if you are in an '80s-heavy-metal-video-babe mood, then you should pile on all the fakes that you own, studs, spikes, rhinestones, scarves, and multiple silver feather earrings. But if you are dressing in homage to the classics . . . Carolyn Bessette Kennedy, Jackie O, and Audrey Hepburn, then, you must remove everything and put on only one special item, maybe a pair of real diamond stud earrings, and a huge pair of tortoiseshell sunglasses.

Or if you are not in homage to anyone but yourself, put on whatever makes you feel your outfit is complete . . . yet NOT overdone, you want to be a standout, not look like you just pulled off a heist at Claire's. We Pesky divas do loathe the "Less is more" theory, because sometimes more IS more, but I do believe that wearing tons of accessories simply to show them off to your friends can make you appear, well, cheap (sorry, dahhlings). I admire a girl's choice of jewelry more when she wears it like it's a piece special to her, like a good luck charm. This makes a more memorable statement, than just putting on your jewelry box.

I have a simple technique for sorting through all those tangled up boxes full o' accessories that you never wear . . . To see if they fit into your wardrobe scheme, lay every accessory you own out on your floor, or on your bed (this means all jewelry, scarves, belts, shoes, purses, hats, and tights). Now get ready to move into a costume designer mode.

Hold things up to each other, try everything on, see what shoes are flattering to your dresses, which costume jewelry you'd love to wear more often, how your grandma's vintage scarf ties in with the colors of your fave groovy pants . . . be picky. Like Hollywood costume designer Edith Head once said, you must remember to keep only in your closet the pieces that enliven and glamify your movie. What good is it to hoard tons of items that will never see the light of day? Give them to someone who will wear them, or sell them to the nearest resale shop, and buy yourself some accessories that you *will* wear. *Hollywood Sparkle*

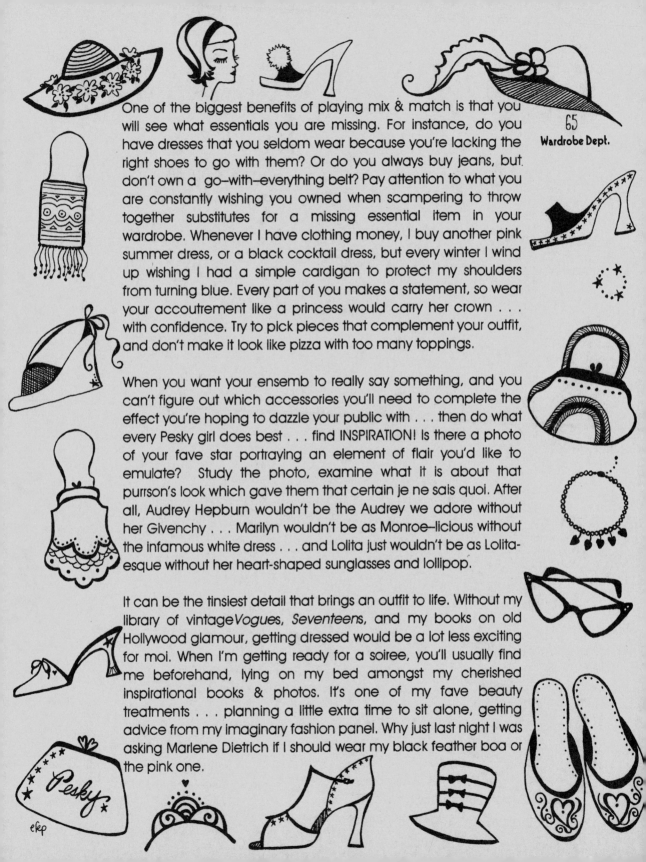

One of the biggest benefits of playing mix & match is that you will see what essentials you are missing. For instance, do you have dresses that you seldom wear because you're lacking the right shoes to go with them? Or do you always buy jeans, but don't own a go–with–everything belt? Pay attention to what you are constantly wishing you owned when scampering to throw together substitutes for a missing essential item in your wardrobe. Whenever I have clothing money, I buy another pink summer dress, or a black cocktail dress, but every winter I wind up wishing I had a simple cardigan to protect my shoulders from turning blue. Every part of you makes a statement, so wear your accoutrement like a princess would carry her crown . . . with confidence. Try to pick pieces that complement your outfit, and don't make it look like pizza with too many toppings.

When you want your ensemb to really say something, and you can't figure out which accessories you'll need to complete the effect you're hoping to dazzle your public with . . . then do what every Pesky girl does best . . . find INSPIRATION! Is there a photo of your fave star portraying an element of flair you'd like to emulate? Study the photo, examine what it is about that purrson's look which gave them that certain je ne sais quoi. After all, Audrey Hepburn wouldn't be the Audrey we adore without her Givenchy . . . Marilyn wouldn't be as Monroe–licious without the infamous white dress . . . and Lolita just wouldn't be as Lolita-esque without her heart-shaped sunglasses and lollipop.

It can be the tinsiest detail that brings an outfit to life. Without my library of vintage *Vogue*s, *Seventeen*s, and my books on old Hollywood glamour, getting dressed would be a lot less exciting for moi. When I'm getting ready for a soiree, you'll usually find me beforehand, lying on my bed amongst my cherished inspirational books & photos. It's one of my fave beauty treatments . . . planning a little extra time to sit alone, getting advice from my imaginary fashion panel. Why just last night I was asking Marlene Dietrich if I should wear my black feather boa or the pink one.

My collaged homage to Anna Sui

My Interview with
ANNA SUI

I was first graced by Anna's presence in 1994 when I visited her shop in Hollywood. My plan was to drool over her gothic purple velvet dresses and save my allowance in hopes of one day being draped in one, but what I was not expecting was to bump into the mistress of glam herself. I bravely introduced myself despite the shaking in my pointy boots and handed her an issue of my 'zine. Apparently she dug it because a few months later she asked me to design tee shirts for two of her collections! Could you just die? To call Anna simply a "fashion designer" would be too vague. She's more like a magical costume maker, or the fairy godmother of fantasy frocks. She designs not only for girls, but for goddesses, glam rockers, flappers, ice princesses, baby dolls, French '60s folk songstresses, gingerbread milkmaids, and gold dust women. Her fannettes include swanky dolls such as Courtney Love, Christina Ricci, Madonna, Cher, Gwen Stefani, and moi of course. So, now allow me to introduce to you my fave Pesky fashion designer of all time . . . The epic **Anna Sui!**

"A little glitter goes a long way"—Anna Sui

Where did your movie begin? My life was always like a fairy tale, where I always dreamt about being a fashion designer. Not that I ever really understood what it meant to be a designer, but that was what I wanted to be since I was four years old. I would tell everybody, but all my aunts and uncles would say, "But you're so smart! you could be a doctor," but I'd say, "Please, no!" It wasn't until I started working that I even understood what a fashion designer was. I'd always just had this idea in my head that I wanted to make beautiful clothes.

So, you just instinctively knew at four that this was going to be your destiny? I guess so. When I was around six I was at this boys house. . . we were using his army men, his older brother was also playing with us, and suddenly we had turned the army into the Academy Awards! We were making tissue paper dresses, and we set it all up like the awards show, and just played that for hours. So that's when I really decided what I wanted to do . . . design clothes for movie stars! The older brother called me a couple of weeks ago. He's in the movie business now, and he called to say that it's so funny that both of us achieved our dream.

Were your parents supportive in helping you to fulfill your dream of becoming a fashion designer? In a Chinese family the boys are more important, so I think my parents never expected me to do anything but be this frivolous party girl that spent a lot of money on clothes, and then get married. I don't think they ever thought I was gonna be a career person. When I had decided to go to Parsons {School of Design} my mother couldn't understand it. She said, "Why do you want to be a dressmaker?" And my father just said, "Oh my god! It's such an expensive school." I don't think they really got it. But now that I've achieved what I have, I don't think they could be prouder of me. They're at every fashion show and they have been since the very beginning, and my father probably knows the press people better than I do.

Do you have any Sui—blings? I have two brothers. They're both stock brokers. My older brother was valedictorian of the class, the smartest person in the school, and everyone always talked about him . . . I was only known as Bob Sui's younger sister. So I felt like I rode through school on his coattails.

Did you express yourself through your wardrobe as a teen?
I guess so, 'cuz I wore feather boas, glitter makeup, and I loved platform shoes. I knew I was going to end up in New York City, since I was accepted to Parsons at sixteen. So I knew a few years ahead of time where I was going to college, and my heart was already in New York at that point.

Since you loved to parade around in feathers and all that jazz, how did your peers react to your fabulocity at such an early age? Well, I was voted best dressed when I was a junior, then I changed schools and didn't know many people!, so at that point I wasn't really concerned about peer pressure because I knew my future was awaiting me in New York. I took a lot of art classes in high school after I had accomplished what I wantedby getting accepted by my dream college. My friends were mostly very artsy, and I fit into that category.

So you chose schools where you knew you'd find fellow feather boa wearers, and wouldn't feel alienated . . . wow! You got off easy compared to the reaction *my* feather boas got me! Do you have a special Anna mantra to inspire all my Pesky girls? I always say "LIVE YOUR DREAM" and I know that's what's always gotten me through the hard times. I think that determination and focus are what got me where I am, and I think that they're really important. Like when I was trying to get a job one summer, I remember going to this wig shop in a mall. The woman was saying to me, "You don't know how to do hair," and I said, "Well, I know how to do hair better than you do!," and she just thought I was some stupid little kid, but I knew inside that I was right, 'cuz I saw how bad her wigs looked. I always knew what I was capable of, and you've gotta have determination to show what you can do.

People used to tell me that doing a fanzine would never lead to anything. I've always felt the doubt of others added fuel to my fire. Now when people tell me I "can't" do something, that's when I think, "Oh yeah? I'll show you!" My favorite thing is when somebody tells me it can't be done, 'cuz then I want to prove that it can be. Don't take no for an answer, because that's the easiest answer to give . . . you have to be persistent and try every angle, until you're truly satisfied with the fact that it can't be done . . . and I'm *never* satisfied with that. For the Scandinavian fabrics in my fall line, the fabric company told me to go away, and I still kept calling, saying, "Listen, you really have to do this," until finally they gave in. It's just such a great challenge.

What qualities must a friend have to be a part of your cast? I've had my friends for a really long time, so loyalty is really important. The most beautiful experience of my life was my first show, when my friends banded together to pull together that show with no money. Steven Meisel (superstar photographer) and Paul Cavaco (*Vogue* fashion editor) helped me get it organized, Naomi Campbell and Linda Evangelista helped me get all the models, and they also got me Garren and Francois Nars for hair and makeup. Then they got all the press to come. So at the end of the show I saw Paul, and we just started crying, and to this day those people still work on my show. Francois doesn't because he has his cosmetics line, but we're still good friends, and Linda doesn't 'cuz she won't do shows anymore, but Naomi still opens and closes my show. I couldn't ask for better friends.

What does being a Pesky Meddling Girl mean to you? It's never accepting no for an answer, being a mover and a shaker, really changing things, and making them the way you dream them to be.

Since "life is a movie" . . . what would the title of yours be, on a glittering marquee? It has to be *Living My Dream*. Sometimes I sit back and think, "WOW! Look what I've accomplished," especially since the launch of my perfume and cosmetics. People tell me how the stuff is selling in Japan and all over the world . . . It's a long way from Detroit!

What is your theme tune? "Child of Moon" by The Rolling Stones.

My movie's message is spreading Pesky-ness to all the girls on the planet. What is your movie's message? My favorite thing in a movie is when I experience something new that I could've never dreamed possible, because it's so beautiful or romantic . . . and I hope that I can bring something to people so they can feel that same way. Through my next collection, my cosmetics, or it could be a piece of jewelry I've designed. Something that makes somebody happy because it's a new experience for them.

When the "Finis" curtain comes down upon your life, what would you like it to say?
The dream goes on . . .

We luv you Anna!

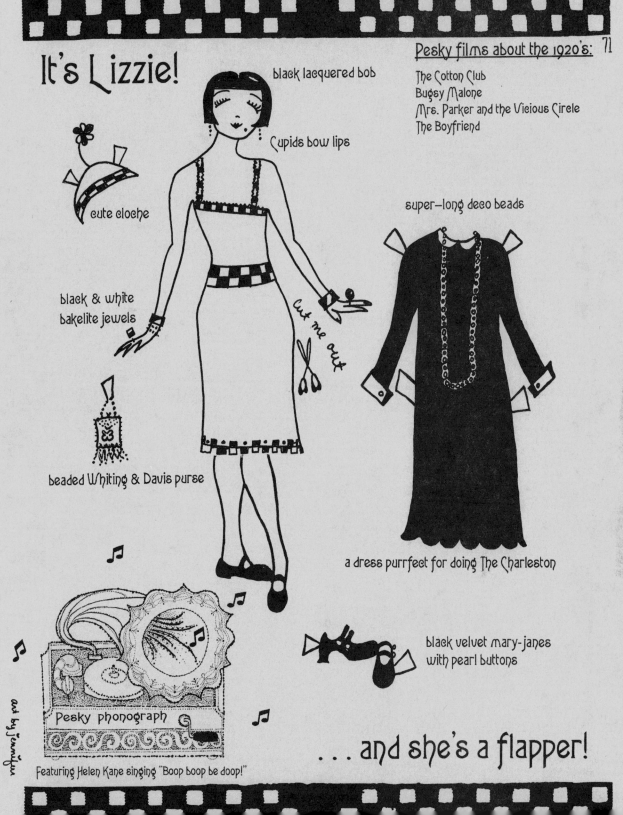

It's Lizzie!

The Cotton Club
Bugsy Malone
Mrs. Parker and the Vicious Circle
The Boyfriend

black lacquered bob

Cupids bow lips

cute cloche

super-long deco beads

black & white
bakelite jewels

cut me out

beaded Whiting & Davis purse

a dress purrfect for doing The Charleston

Pesky phonograph

black velvet mary-janes
with pearl buttons

art by Jennifer

Featuring Helen Kane singing "Boop boop be doop!"

. . . and she's a flapper!

72

Me in the original pink gown Marilyn Monroe wore in *Gentlemen Prefer Blondes* !

Special thanks to Douglas Little & Travilla

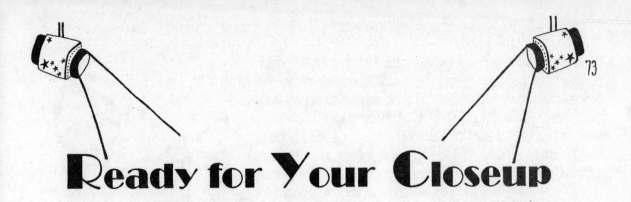

Ready for Your Closeup

Makeup delivers a message to your audience . . . It tells them that you won't be ignored. It is an expression of your inner girl, and depending how you apply your violet glitter eyeliner, blood burgundy lipstick, or sky blue mascara, you are creating a lasting image that people will remember you by. So if you dig the au naturel look, don't be surprised if hippie boys want to take you daisy picking . . . or if you love Twiggy falsies, white lipstick, and ironing your hair, mod boys may invite you to go go-go-ing on the Sunset Strip . . . or if you adore black lip soot, evil noir eyeliner, and glue-on vampire bites, well, you can guess what kind of crowd will slither in your direction . . . The image = YOU.

But on the other manicured hand . . .
True Beauty has nothing to do with makeup. It's about self-esteem, self discipline, and creativity. It's about making the most out of everything you've got, being creative, and making sure you're making a bee-ooo-tee-ful life for yourself. Those should be your top beautific priorities, not "How can I cover up what's wrong with me or weirdly different about me?" Another tip I'd like to pass on to you is never be ashamed that you dig staring in the mirror, primping, and experimenting daily with various beauty routines. This only adds fun to your life, enables you to play sorceress with your appearance, improves your self image, and gives you that ultra-important moment of the day to say "Hello, Gorgeous!" All I ask is that you admire not only your girly gifts, but your flaws as well. When I think about all the women I find to be devastatingly gorgeous, it's usually because they are different from all the cookie-cutter blondes we see Hollywood worshiping. The women I find stunning are unusual: Isabella Rossellini with her crooked front tooth, Cyndi Lauper with her half-moon-shaped eyes, Christina Ricci with her gothic doll face, Molly Ringwald with lips poutier than Mick Jagger, Greta Garbo with eyelids so vast you could pen a novel on them, and my mom who is voluptuous and proud of it! Who would you rather look like? . . . The totally perfect blonde with the flawless bod who replaced Suzanne Somers on *Three's Company*? No, I can't remember her name either (I've already made my point.) Or someone cool, unforgettable, and original like Bette Davis, with her husky voice, exaggerated lips, and blue eyes so legendary that rock songs are written in homage to them?

☆ *Let Your Beauty be Seen* ☆

If you were to ask most boys which hottie they'd prefer (excluding the ones who are still getting over the whole puberty thing, which I've observed actually lasts until they are about thirty), they'd most likely say whichever one wears hot pants, tube tops, and poses for posters usually adorning wall of a mechanic's office (see: *Three's Company* bimbo). But not all the cool boys I know (you'll meet some too, just look for the arty ones, or the cute nerds taking accounting), they all worship the witty wisdom-spouting siren that is big peepers Bette Davis. She's a much sexier and intriguing creature to any cool boy. Purrfection is a bore. Being a hardcore beauty is actually very simple. All you have to do is follow my Pesky advice (all of which has been tested true by both my sister, Lizzie, and moi), and live a healthy lifestyle, be a nice purrson, honest, considerate of others, and you'll undoubtably exude a beauteous and peaceful glow that emits from your inside. Happiness really shows on your face, and makes people swarm to you like bees to honey. It's the truth, not just some cheesy hippie philosophy.

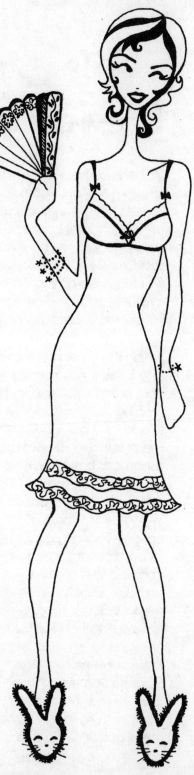

So my advice to you is instead of covering or camouflaging what's different about you . . . try and figure out how to accentuate it so you'll stand out in a crowd. The goal for every PESKY diva is NEVER to blend. Even if you've taken the chance to really be seen, and people are responding negatively, then that only means you possess something most waitresses in Hollywood would pay cash money for . . . STAR QUALITY! This is something you share with Madonna herself . . . not everybody loves her, some may even say they hate her, but one thing they can't stop doing is watching. Most people just have auras surrounding them of being "invisible," but not you my dear . . . you're in the limelight 24/7 . . . bask in it's glow, and don't give a hoot what other people think, because you're the star, baby, and you call the shots on how you feel about your day-to-day performances.

ekp

Powderpuff Girl :

Looking After Your Skin—Star-Style

Before we discuss makeup, you must first start with a clean canvas on which to paint. Concealer can do wonders, but let's shoot for a flawless face anyhow. And the best way to achieve movie star looks is through purrfect skin care. The secret? Read on, dahhling!

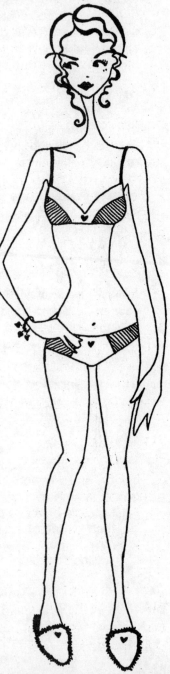

Jennifur's Guide to Glammy and Glowing Skin—

Since I live in Hollywood and have my mug tended to by reputable technicians of Oscar winner skin, my advice is worth a pretty penny . . . but you won't have to shell out a fortune, I'll gladly share my secrets with you, doll.

Gently, gently . . . your face needs a vacation—My facialist at a superswanky spa in Hollywood, has taught me to treat my skin as if it were a newborn baby's. When I went in for my very first facial, I was a complexion disaster. I had been attacking my pores like a terrorist, buying every product that would profess to make my zits disappear. I had also gone previously to a dermatologist, whose directions I ignored, and was impatiently spreading harsh treatments on my face twice a day to clear up my skin, and hopefully my self-image too.

By the time I arrived for the facial, I was irritated and red as a tomato. I had come to believe that was just my skin's normal state. She taught me that when it comes to your face, less is best, especially if you have sensitive skin like mine. I threw away all my bogus products, and she got me started on a supergentle cleanser called Cetaphil (also worshiped by glam girls Chloe Sevigny and Liv Tyler), insisted I wear sun block every day, and turned me on to aloe vera as moisturizer. If I have a whopper of a zit, I apply only a Q-tip dot of my prescription medication. I think lots of girls get caught up in the aggressive skin-spanking pattern I did. It's as if we don't put any trust into our own bodies to heal our faces. Usually all our skin needs is a little love, trust, and a permanent vacation from our own abuse. It's time to treat your face like the delicate butterfly that it is.

Never touch your face—I don't care if you have a tiny volcano on your forehead displaying a neon sign flashing "POP ME" . . . never touch your face! There are more pimple-producing oils on your fingers than you could possibly imagine. If you have an itch, just make sure you wash your hands before you go for it, or do what I do, and use a soft tissue to pat it. Once I stopped poking , my skin got noticeably clearer. It just takes a lil' self-control.

Don't smoke! Smoking announces to the world that you're too stupid to stop doing things that will eventually kill you . . . not to mention give you lip wrinkles, dull skin, gross breath, and yellow teeth. How glam is that?

Room service, please—You should be using your own towels and washcloths to dry your face. Try not to use towels that other people have dried their hands on, these still store oils that could cause a potential breakout. I would also suggest washing your personal face towel after every third use, or more often if possible. NOTE: Harsh laundry detergents can also be irritative. I buy a gentler, natural detergent at my local health food store and wash my towels and delicate dresses in it.

Pet nice—When towel-drying your face after a wash, DON'T rub dry, DO pat lightly. If you are roughly drying your face, what you may not realize is that you are actually exfoliating your face, probably two times a day even! No wonder your skin gets irritated. Exfoliation should be left to a professional. Remember to pet nice, and if it so moves you . . . invest in a supersoft towel.

Always remove your war paint before sleepy time—There are NO excuses! I don't ever want to hear you say "But I'm too tired" or "Just this once won't hurt" . . . it will. If you skimp on cleansing all the clogging foundation gunk out of your pores every eve, you will pay the price in lovely things like blackheads and volcanic pimples. Is it worth all that drama?

Frosty the Snowy Skin Girl says . . . In wintertime, when you turn on the heater, your skin is being drained of its natural moisture. An easy way to solve this without having to buy a humidifier is to place a bowl of water next to your bed. This technique keeps moisture in the air. You could even study this fact for the next science fair.

Be a sun-blockin' soul sista—You must apply sunscreen every day before leaving your house, even when it's cloudy! I know this sounds square, but trust moi . . . When you're forty and appear not a day older than eighteen, you'll be sending me roses . . . And all your shrively Coppertone girl friends will wish they bummed a lil' SPF 30 from you. Leaving the house sans sunscreen will run you at the likely risk of getting skin cancer. This has already happened to several of my twenty-something Malibu babe friends, and they've all agreed that their tubular tans were not worth the excruciating pain of having spots removed. They wish they'd stayed goth/Lily Munster pale like me. But If you are having a problem with this due to your wanting to look like an exotic hula girl, then try any of the chic new self-tanners available. so, block, block away! It's our fountain of youth. **Attention, all metropolitan girls:** Sun block also protects your face from all the smog, pollutants, and general dirt flying around in the gross city air.

Atomizer & Eve—It's lovely to mist your face with cold water during the day. Skin loves drinking water as much as the daisies do, and it's a nonmessy way to moisturize, since it mystically evaporates. Evian makes fab purse-size atomizers, but they're expensive, so do what I do; buy a tiny travel spray bottle, and fill it with filtered tap water. It's also a dream during air travel.

Spoil yourself when necessary, I'm giving you permission—I held off going to a dermatologist and facialist for ten years of my irritated skin due to the fact that I felt it was too extravagant a cost. But let me ask you this, my dahhlings . . . What price is your self-image worth to you? This is the question my mom asked me one day after listening to me cry and complain about my complexion for my whole teen term. I desperately wanted my level of self-confidence to improve, so I could go just one full day without wondering if I was ugly. I knew there was more to life than "Jennifur's skin crises," so I took the plunge into my wallet, and made the necessary calls. I can't tell you how much it has improved my self-image, even just knowing that I did something to better myself. I used to think that I would be considered self-centered for splurging on my skin, but it was actually one of the most generous things I've done, considering all my friends were totally sick of hearing me complain. Your self- image is ALWAYS worth the investment; in fact, it's priceless, so make sure you spend all the time and moolah that it takes in order to find that necessary level of self-love. Stop bitching about everything that's wrong with you unless you are willing to actually DO something about it. Pamper yourself, do all the research it takes to understand your appearance, you'll never know until you try. Maybe then you'll dig yourself to the fullest, like you should have all along.

Calgon, take me away!—Stress = zits. It's a fact. So take a deep yoga breath, and let all your worries roll over that nervous yet pretty head of yours. If you find that you are indeed a stress case (like moi!), then for your body's sake, and your face's . . . find something that relaxes you. Most girls don't give themselves that totally needed hour of alone time every single day. It's cathartic to have some time just for you, to assess all the things that occurred that day, and to keep all your goals and feelings in perspective. Don't be too hard on yourself. Sneak in one moment every day to pamper your girly-ness within, even when you are having a superhectic week. Think of lovely things to chant to yourself every night as you fall asleep, and believe in the fact that a healthy and relaxed self leads to healthy and relaxed skin. My favorite end of week wind-down is to take a steamy bubble bath with Origins Sleep-enhancing milk bath and just think in silence. Another great de-stresser is finding a peaceful spot in your backyard, or neighborhood coffee shop, and just read. Whether you're reading *Teen People* or Jane Austen matters not. All that matters is that you give yourself that much needed YOU time.

Yes, all of you — *pamper all of you*

zzzzzzzzzz

What is your fave YOU time of the day: _____

_____

ekp

Once your skin is squeaky-clean, it's time to get camera-ready . . .

Makeup is my bag, baby!

Here, for all you teen luvlies, are my current fave war paint picks . . .

Everything by Anna Sui—Her entire line is so much fun that I usually exit the house looking like LaToya Jackson. My fave items are her pink doll blush, fuscia glitter lipstick #001, glitter eyegloss (I use it in my hair too!), the clear purple lipgloss #200, and Anna Sui perfume (which smells so good I almost trashed my bottle of Boudoir by Vivienne Westwood! Well, almost). Not to mention that Anna's items are rose scented! Holy girly girdles!

Anything by Chanel—It makes me feel so superfancy to pull out my black lacquer compacts adorned with those legendary double C's. I may not be able to afford a Chanel suit, but I can sometimes afford the luxury of owning chanel makeup. My faves are the sparkly pink powderlights and the "lip blush" in Lucifer Kissed.

Revlon's black Colorstay mascara is the wickedest lashifier ever! Every time I blink, I practically have to say "Excuse me." Put it on over false lashes, and you're liable to poke someone's eye out!

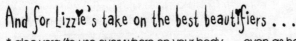

Andrea makes my fave false lashes. They make me feel like the '60s MODel Jean Shrimpton (or The Shrimp as she was known back in the day). My style is #33 brown.

Bonne Bell's flavored lipgloss—These have been assisting girls during smooching sessions since your mom was your age. My current fave flav is chocolate milk.

P.esky **S.**ecret: These companies do not test on animals . . . so, Meeeowww!

And for Lizzie's take on the best beautifiers . . .

* aloe vera (to use everywhere on your body . . . even as hair gel!)
* Vaseline (to soften hands and feet while you sleep at night)
* Anna Sui's glitter mascara (when a boy looks into your eyes, he'll really see stars!)
* Body Shop's Almond Nut Body Butter
* Anna Sui's red nail polish (It has a lovely bottle, and never chips!)

Do tell . . . what cherished products are in your makeup bag, dahhling?

_____

_____

_____

ekp

A Reality Check for Your Fabulous Face

This may give your self-confidence a lil' boost . . . I grew up in Hollywood, land of Malibu Barbies and plastic surgery princesses. I see a supermodel a week (No kidding!), and spotting Oscar nominees is a daily occurrence for me . . . but they all share one thing not shown in magazines or on film . . . FLAWS! An example? I once found myself standing next to one very infamous über-model who photographs like a Grecian statue, but in person she looked regular (but slightly taller). Her hair was all greasy, and she had a face full of blemishes! Needless to say, I liked her more after that. Airbrushing is the hugest conspiracy to us girls, but I just wanted to expose the truth, so that you can rest assured . . . models DO get zits too.

PESKY THINGS TO DO:

If you have a volcanic zit threatening to ruin your day, use my favorite trick . . . Glue a rhinestone using a dab of eyelash glue over the blemish, and voilà! Instant beauty mark!

Refuse to ask yourself any of the following very un-Pesky questions . . .
"Do I look ugly today?"
"Does my makeup look bad?"
"Do I look bad in this?"
"Is he going to notice my zits?"
I will tell you, as your new true friend, the answer to all these questions is simply . . . "NO!"

Your skin is your body's largest organ. It's your shell, and no two shells are alike, so customize your skin regimen to fit your lifestyle. It is the one-of-a-kind mannequin with which to display all your costumes, and display all that is YOU. Treat it well, and wear it with Pesky pride.

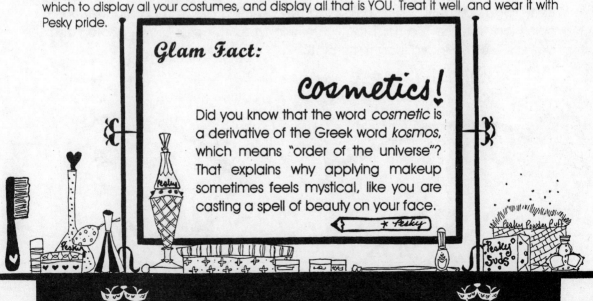

Glam Fact:

cosmetics!

Did you know that the word *cosmetic* is a derivative of the Greek word *kosmos*, which means "order of the universe"? That explains why applying makeup sometimes feels mystical, like you are casting a spell of beauty on your face.

★ Pesky

Your movie is showing live, in person, so i've collected some fabulous makeup tips for you! I purrsonally guarantee them to be de-voom!

this lovely newcomer shows you how to steal the scene in real as well as "reel" life...with stellar supporting performances by match-the-mood eyelashes.

How to Achieve Super-Flirty Pesky Peepers

FALSIES . . . FRET NOT! . . . and no, I'm not speaking of boobies . . . false lashes, silly! They are sooo Twiggy, and totally Marlo Thomas too (*That Girl* on Nick at Night). Once you've mastered your lashes, you can start adding crazy things to them with lash glue, like feathers & sequins. The fun just never stops!

MODEL TIP—If you have squinty, half-moon-shaped eyes like moi, and want to make them appear huge & doelike, or innocent '60s & Twiggy-like . . . use a white liner on the inside of your bottom lash line. I use "White" by Make-up Forever. It's groovy!

GIVE YOUR PEEPERS A BREAK—My mom told me recently about the most stunning lady in her neighborhood growing up, whose beauty secret was not to remove her eye makeup every night, but to wait until the next morning when it comes off in a gentler fashion. After all, pulling at your peepers every day can't be good. Remember to pamper them, too, with an eye gel. My fave is "Eye Specialist" by Prescriptives. It's like a fab night's sleep in a tube.

ATTENTION ALL FAIR HAIRED-BEAUTIES—If you have anything lighter than jet black Betty Page hair, then you should probably be using brown mascara instead of noir. Black can be too harsh on lighter skin types . . . plus brown photographs better (Cindy Crawford taught me that).

Have the Witching Eyes *of the Movie Stars* Tonight!

Hey! Lucious Lips Up For Grabs!

While brushing your teeth, brush your lips lightly as well. It slightly swells them, giving them a pouty look, brings out their natural redness, and eliminates dead skin. Follow with some nourishing lip-gloss, and you're utterly kissable. Beauty Beware: Brush your lips only once a day. Any more will chap your pout!

Layer supershiny flavored lip gloss over your dark matte lipsticks.

To avoid embarrassing lipstick-on-the-teeth scenarios, rub a dot of Vaseline on your teeth before going out. This trick is often used by celebs.

Fun Tips For Fancy Nails

Paint your fingy nails a different color than your toes. Color coordinating can be a bore sometimes. Try painting your fingys a candy apple red and your toes a hot fuscia pink. These colors weren't meant to go together, but we love breaking the rules, don't we? Pink polish makes your nails look like little edible candies.

Glue crazy things to them! Like gaudy sequins, flashy rhinestones, star stickers, or tiny photos of your friends. Whatever you can possibly fit!

SATURDAY IS "MANICURE DAY"

Smell So Delicious He May Try to Take a Bite!

Become an overnight parfumier! Buy scented hippie oils, and mix them to create your own custom scent. I was experimenting recently and found that these oils smell heavenly together; Patchouli & Johnson's baby powder, and vanilla & orchid. You can even use things like crushed rose petals in your mix .

IT'S NO LONGER THE SEVENTEENTH CENTURY! Always wear deodorant . . . but you knew that already. Do try using a healthy brand though. One that doesn't list aluminum as an ingredient. it's been suspected to cause Alzheimer's.

What Is your signature perfume or scent?

Lovely You

Where's that smile?

_____

List all of your favorite smells:

_____

_____

_____

ekp

81

BEAUTIFICALLY PESKY THINGS TO DO:

REMEMBER THAT brains are better than beauty, even though you *ARE* bee-oo-tee-ful—The wardrobe and war paint you choose can make you look the part you'd like to play, but it can't replace the talent you need to actually play it. I have a good example of the brainy asset over perfection . . . In the lame flick *The Truth about Cats and Dogs*, a supposedly "ugly" yet super-smart character (played by goddess-like Janeane Garofalo) is so ashamed of her looks, that when asked on a blind date, she sends her dim-witted but perfect neighbor (Uma Thurman) instead, so she won't have to face the humility that is her face. I didn't buy this story from the minute it began, so to road-test this scenario I asked my boyfriend who he would ask out first. He said (to my holy surprise) that he would ask the dexterous Miss Garofalo out because she could make him laugh and keep him interested. He explained to me that guys don't go chasing intimidating, or high-maintenance girls. They much prefer the ones who would throw on jeans, eat a chili dog in front of you, and not care if their hair gets messed up. He confirmed that any guy who would go straight for beauty over brains would be shallow and not worth dating anyway. And as legendary *Cosmo* editrix Helen Gurley Brown once said, "If I had to choose beauty or brains, I'd take brains, every time."

SIT UP STRAIGHT—Good posture gives you a royal vibe . . . like Audrey Hepburn in *Roman Holiday*. You can be five feet tall like both Clara Bow & Lil' Kim, yet still look worlds above everyone else, just sit up straight!

DON'T be afraid TO experiment with your looks— You are young . . . now's the time to do it. Explore every beauty avenue. Change your hair color, use green mascara, get creative, have a makeover party with your best friends.

SMILE! It's like sunshine through a window to the sweetness in your soul . . . So use it a lot!

she's a doll!

If you RUN OUT of blush . . . use lipstick and rub it in!

DO
your own
THiNG!

Give yourself a new look!

Draw a picture of yourself, or use a photograph. Glue glitter on it, fingerpaint it, collage it . . . see how you'd look with green hair, a nose pierce, or a beauty mark . . . any makeover thing you've ever dreamed of trying!

Angel... or Devil?

BE A SIREN

Glammy–Locks . . . and the Three Barrettes

If you ever get bored with your lifeless locks don't be afraid to try something new! Put them up in loopy Dutch-style braids, sprinkle some craft shop glitter on your head, make an Erykah Badu–esque turban of fun fur from your local fabric store, slick it into a sleek Madonna Blonde Ambition-era ponytail, for Shirley Temple corkscrew curls use steam rollers (they don't cause damage!), wear fancy prom up-'dos with jeans, play hair salon with your friends and whatever you end up looking like is how you leave the house . . . the possibilities are endless! Remember those life-size Barbie heads you could give makeovers to? Well, pretend your head is one of those. How boring would it have been to have just left your Barbie noggin untouched and unglamorized? So don't get caught in the trap of styling your hair the same way every day because it's convenient . . . *have fun, tiara on, wig out!*

My tips for making the most out of your 'do.

shampoo

If you have normal or oily hair, shampoo every day—I hate to be the one to ruin the illusion for you, but . . . I can always tell when a girl has skipped a day of washing her hair. And if you are indeed one of the offenders, remember that any dirt or oil on your locks winds up on your skin, clogging pores (ultra-gross!). Besides, the squeaky-clean, shiny-haired girl is oh so '70s, disco, Brooke Shields—era glam. You'll look like you "just stepped out of the salon" if you keep your hair as immaculate as your face.

your hair

Alternate between two different shampoos and two different conditioners—Do this every other day or weekly. The reasoning being that your hair, oddly enough, gets used to your usual product and doesn't respond like it should anymore. Your hair is very similar in purrsonality to you, it likes excitement every so often, and what better a way to throw a surprise soiree for your locks than with some new 'poo! Doing the product switch will add more bounce & glimmer to occasionally dull hair.

Wigs are our friends—I can't even count on my pink manicured nails on just how many occasions I'd been in a total coif crisis, and my magical wigs or falls came to the rescue. Every Pesky girl should own at least one wig. It doesn't even matter if it's a $5 cheapy one . . . it can make all the difference in boosting your purrsonality on a night when your coif is uncooperative, or you feel Madonna-chameleon-like. It's also fab for when you decide to do something regrettably drastic to your natural 'do during moments of teen rebellion. A less "wiggy" option for the girl who likes a more natural look is to clip on a fall. These were the necessary accessories in the '60s and early '70s, and it's a swatch of hair that matches your color, which you just clip on for an instant Bond girl look. These work miracles and look MOD-ly gorgeous. Mine always makes me feel like a go-go dancer. So get wiggy with it!

Here are some purrfectly Pesky hair products:

Kiehl's—These people are shrineworthy. Everything they produce is natural and animal friendly to boot. I can't blow dry without their Shine 'n Lite Groom leave-in styling creme. It took my hair from crispy heavy metal to something resembling spun gold. Use this hair goo of the stars!

Manic Panic—My high school rebellion would've been a bore without the shocking power of Flamingo Pink vegetable dye. It's classic punk color stuff, which washes totally out in about a month (unless your hair is really porous, then not at all). Just give mom & dad a warning before pulling a Marilyn Manson out of your hat. **P**.esky **S**.ecret: Washing your hair with cold water makes your color vibrant longer. Warm water will make it fade quicker.

Colored Halloween hair spray—It comes in the most lovely Day-Glo psychedelic colors imaginable . . . and your parents will cut you some slack because it says adieu in one wash. I'd love to have pink streaks à la Cyndi Lauper right now . . . excuse me . . . *Psssst* . . .

Your Film's Budget

Save your dough . . . dye at home!

I dye my locks at home so I don't have to sit in a stuffy salon all sunny day while they put stuff on my roots that actually costs $9 at the beauty supply. Plus, what's more girly than doing your toes whilst watching Fashion Television and eating Ben & Jerry's while waiting for your hair to process. Save your moolah (buy a new frock with the $$$ you save), invite some friends over, blast some Blondie, and perform your very own coif wizardry. **The Smart me. The Glamorous me. The Thrifty me!**

Glue a photo here of your dream hair 'do:

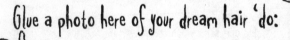

Dreamy drawing by DougLas Little

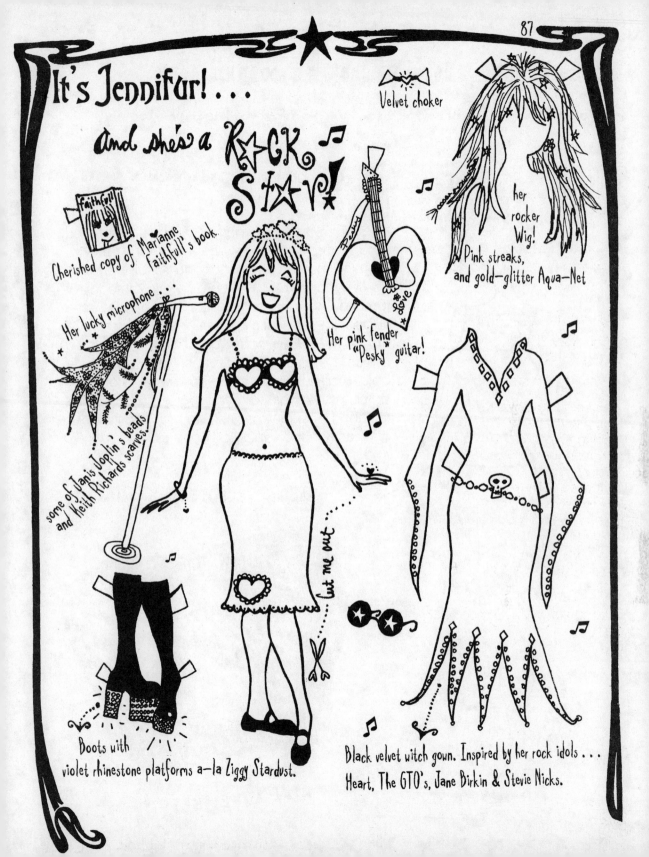

It's Jennifur!...

and she's a R★CK-St★v!

Velvet choker

her rocker Wig! Pink streaks, and gold-glitter Aqua-Net

Cherished copy of Marianne Faithfull's book.

Her lucky microphone...

Her pink Fender "Pesky" guitar!

some of Janis Joplin's beads and Keith Richards scarves.

Cut me out...

Boots with violet rhinestone platforms a-la Ziggy Stardust.

Black velvet witch gown. Inspired by her rock idols... Heart, The GTO's, Jane Birkin & Stevie Nicks.

Getting the Star Treatment

Follow this tip and not only will you look glam, but you'll feel glam too!

"My secret is positive thinking and no drinking."—Mae West

If liquor or drugs are part of your diet, then you should absolutely try to veto them from now on. Anything that intoxicates your purrsonality is totally un-Pesky, and you'll end up as no star of today or tomorrow, but as a has-been reminiscent of a *Diff'rent Strokes* cast member, or as a tragic profile on *E! True Hollywood Stories*. Start anew . . . become a clean teen, and only then will you be able to be truly Pesky to the point where star-glam status just exudes from your pores. I learned this first hand after almost destroying my health, looks, and sanity in the vapid Hollywood club-kid scene.

"Take drugs? . . . I am drugs!"—Salvador Dalí

WHO WOULDN'T BE A

Glamour Girl

WHEN IT COSTS SO LITTLE?

FOR THAT HEAVENLY LOOK OF STAR-LIKE LOVELINESS

ekp

Craft Services

You'll need lots of nourishment while working on the movie that is your life. So, here are some tips on eating like the star that you are:

I don't believe in diets, the thing I *do* believe makes you look and feel svelte is simply living healthily. Try paying total attention to what your body is trying to tell you, including how it reacts to all the different kinds of foods you are fueling it with. For instance . . . if you've noticed that every time you eat red meat you feel bloated afterward . . . stop eating red meat. I know it's harder to do than it sounds, because it's always the food that causes your body to respond funky is usually the one you love most to chow, but good health is worth going through the withdrawals of any craving. Your body has subtle ways of telling you it disagrees with your food choices. I ignored the messages my bod was sending me for years, and what did it get me? . . . Many impromptu exits from fab soirees due to yucky stomachaches!

YUM!
YUM! Don't let this type of self-body abuse happen to you! Learn to hear your hot bod's cries for nutritional help. Your body *can* learn to live without the junky things you are now used to munching on. Once I cut out all my achey-stomach culprits, I noticed a drastic difference . . . better skin, more stamina to get through the day, easier time awaking in the once hateful morning, and a sense of self-accomplishment. A good way to exclude something you adore to eat that doesn't make you feel fab afterwards is by learning to substitute. For instance . . . if every time you eat chocolate you've noticed you get a blemish the next day . . . then switch to fruit smoothies or carob desserts. Or if you have a reaction to red meat . . . then cut it out of your diet, but make sure you are getting enough protein by eating lots of chicken (free-range) and fish.

Delicious Plain or Fancy!

It's ultra-easy to eat like a catered-to superstar, all you need learn is how to make a conscious effort every day to eat healthily. Remember to eat like your insides are the banquet tables at the Academy Awards dinner. But if someone happens to offer you an Oreo . . . not to accept would be downright rude!

Pesky fishys, chickies, tomatoes, tater hash . . .
Here's how to eat like a star for very little cash . . .

Some yummy notes on noshing:
How to make a diet dish . . . and be one!

If you want a bod like Madonna or Angelina Jolie . . . eat more green veggies.

Instead of having your chicken, tuna, or burger on bread . . . try it between two lettuce cups. You'll start to feel slimmer instantly!

Substitute dried-banana or apple chips for greasy potato chips.

Cut out soda! It messes with your metabolism, and turns pearly whites quite un-pearly.

If you get that four P.M. drained-of-all-energy feeling, don't dismiss it as "low blood sugar" to be cured instantly by a KitKat bar. You are probably just dehydrated and need to drink water. If you still crave a snack after that, then try something healthy like a protein bar.

Start writing down everything you eat. This way you can see what bad things you're eating too often and what nutrients you are lacking.

Don't skip breakfast! It's the most important meal of the day. If you are a get-up-&-go kind of girl, then you should try having a protein shake every morning. Get opinions at your local health food store, or on the Internet, as to which shake is best for you. The shake I prefer is by Genisoy, it's chocolate flavored and I add bananas to it. Yummm

Set snack limits, and don't cheat! I allow myself only ONE trip to Ben & Jerry's a week (Chunky-Monkey rocks!). It's utter torture, but at least I fit in my brown velvet hip-hugger-bell–bottoms, and that's mucho important for my self-esteem.

List here the very un-PESKY foods you chow: _____

_____

List here the Pesky-healthy things you will try to eat more often: _____

_____

Describe your dream meal: _____

_____

If you take extra care of what's on the inside, your outside will get results as well. The Pesky code of health goes like this . . . Lead a hooch-free (except for the occasional glass of pink champagne on ritzy occasions), drug-free (even though I do believe in the legalization of pot for medical purposes), cigarette-free (no exceptions!), fast-food-free (they treat the cows & chickies cruelly) life . . . and you will be a truly glimmering & stunning girl, no doubt about it!

★ Jennifur's Pesky Discosize Workout!

I am the last purrson who should be talking to you about fitness. But I do have a fun way of working out if you, like me, would rather stick pins in your eyes than join a gym. It's the Pesky workout, of course, and it goes a lil' something like this . . .

Get Thin to Music

DERRIERE DARLING

Wait until your parents are out, and pop on a mellow warm-up tune, maybe some Radiohead or Björk. To warm up, you should slowly stretch out your muscles for the entire duration of the song. Move however you want, but be careful. Then, after you feel you're all warmed up, put on a really high-energy album and dance crazy, abandoning all regard for normal body movement. I have found the purrfect album for doing Jennifur's-Pesky-Discocize-workout, and it is the raver fave *Dewdrops in the Garden* by Deee-Lite. If you dance for the entire duration of the album, three times a week, you will have Pamela Lee buns in no time. Just get your heart pumpin' and have some Flashdancin' fun! Break dances like The Robot are also great for your cardiovascular system. The Pesky rule is . . . The lamer the movement, the better the workout!

Suggested Discocizing Tunes:

Midnite Vultures—Beck
Darkdancer—Les Rythmes Digitales
On the Radio—Donna Summer
The Immaculate Collection—Madonna
Off the Wall—Michael Jackson

★ CHEERS FOR CHUBBY

Which sports do you kick tush at?_____

_____

you are beautiful

A YUMMY PESKY THING TO DO

BECOME AN AGUA-holic—Drink eight glasses of water every day. I know it sounds tedious, but there is not one stunning model or actress who drinks any less. If you won't do it for your skin, do it for your health. Your body needs it in order to flush out all it's icky toxins. Your body is like a daisy in the sunshine, needing that special something in order to grow, and what's the necessary bloomin' juice? Agua, darlin'! **P.**esky **S.**ecret: Be a good lil' nature princess and recycle those bottles!

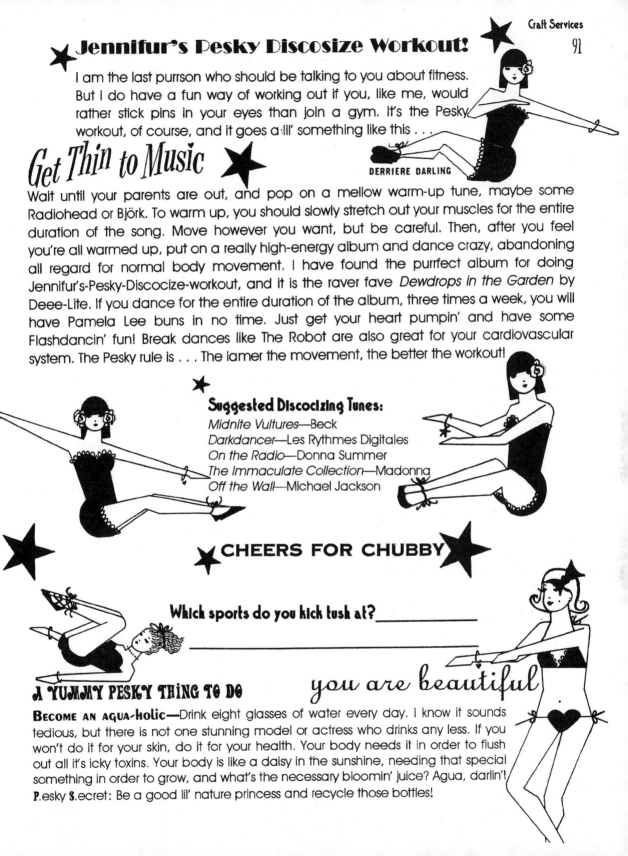

Leading Man

Stop kissing that framed photo of Leonardo and listen up! Boys . . . What can I say? They're cute! . . . and there are lots of them . . . So, I'm here to help you pick the best ones and ditch the doofuses, not to mention dress you in a first–date ensemb so simply de-voom, the dream-babes will be swarming to you like bees to honey! You see, we are blessed with visions of total stone-foxy potential beaus every living day . . . Don't think I would let you down by denying you the lowdown covering everything from "what to wear" to how to spot un-Pesky boys, and (of course) when to let him lay on the ol' smoocheroo. Through juicy stories of my own past purrsonal delves into the fishy waters of the high school crush scene, you will be a dating doyenne in no time, whilst wearing the proper get-up as well!

Lights . . . Camera . . . Attraction!

CASTING CALL: Tall, Dark, and a Hottie

The first thing I'd like you to keep in mind is that dating is a learning experience. We'd love to think it's all just for fun, but when other people's emotions are involved, it's more complex than that. Dating different boys helps you learn about yourself and how you should treat others. Committing to a relationship with a boy you dig, whether it be for a week or a year, will teach you lessons you can use your entire life . . . things *to* do in a relationship and things *not* to do. So even if you think you should beat yourself up for staying with an un-Pesky boy for three valuable years of your junior high existence, don't waste any more time crying over spilled foundation . . . just list the things you learned while you were with the wrong boy. Gaining knowledge resulting from disastrous relationships is priceless, and I believe firmly that having at least one Poopy-not-Pesky beau in your life is an asset. It teaches you exactly what *not* to look for in a babe . . . and knowledge is power, my kitty.

Pesky Meddling Men Possess the Following Features . . .

- ♥ A clean-cut persona
- ♥ An open mind
- ♥ A fuzzy "boyfriend" cardigan that he drapes around you on chilly nights.
- ♥ A trustworthy nature
- ♥ Mom taught him to always treat you like a lady, and he actually listened.
- ♥ An extensive knowledge of punk & jazz music
- ♥ Great friends who you dig spending time with
- ♥ Buys you girly gifts often
- ♥ Has a set of hot wheels, but drives slowly with you in the car
- ♥ Not afraid to dance at parties
- ♥ Makes sure no one bumps into you at concerts
- ♥ Respects your house rules
- ♥ Makes you laugh till you have to pee

What Pesky purrsonality traits would your leading man need to possess?

_____

_____

_____

_____

_____

_____

Date **D**arlings

GIRLS . . .
PLEASE DO MAKE PASSES AT NERDS WHO WEAR GLASSES

When scoping the world for nice boys to snog . . . keep your eye out for NERDS! Forget about those pretty, popular hunky boys, nerdy nerds are très geek chic! In my experience, they make better boyfriends, and are smarter to boot! They are shy and self-conscious, so when they find out you dig them, they go to extreme levels to give you the sun and the moon. They walk around thinking things like "Gee, she really likes me. I'm the luckiest boy in the world." They actually crave commitment and are genuinely proud of you when you work really hard on projects. They will run out at midnight to buy you an emergency box of Tampax, and won't be ashamed to do it, either! They are into more creative dates than the average Joe . . . Things like foreign films, museums, vintage car races, and trips to Office Depot thrill them to no end! It's also entertaining to get them excited about anything, most of them develop a cute stutter when they get nervous. They are computer geniuses, so when you're together you can pretend he's Anthony Michael Hall and you're Kelly LeBrock in *Weird Science, AND* they can't see your pimples without their glasses on (what could be better?) Most girls like to give their nerds a wardrobe makeover, but I don't believe in that . . . Dork couture has got it goin' on! (Unless they need help with their hygiene, then by all means make suggestions.) With my nerd beau I like to capitalize on his studiousness. I think it's sexy. I beg him to get his pants hemmed slightly too short, and to wear argyle socks. Good places to scout specs wearers are; at any record shop selling *Computer World* by Kraftwerk on vinyl, or hidden in office cubicles everywhere. Good luck finding your true geek love!

ekp

Another thing every Pesky dating doyene should do once she's in the presence of a worshipful boy (and he *should* be acting worshipful of you) is to set rules. Boys may go along with it if you are some party girl who has no curfew, and likes to get wasted, but all you are doing is showing them that you aren't the type of girl who deserves a commitment. He will soon be dreaming of sweet girls, the kind who leave him wanting more, so set some standards. By this I mean making your own curfew, especially on school nights. Tell him you can go dancing, or to the movies, but you must be home by the time you and your agents have set. Boys love girls who have this kind of discipline with themselves. After all . . . if you are abiding by no one's rules and neglecting all the things you need to get done on time, then why would you seem reliable or responsible to him?

Other rules you can make with him are things like . . . having to meet your parents before taking you out on the first date, making sure he doesn't pressure you to go out with him on nights you promised to spend time with your friends, whatever you think is applicable to the kind of lifestyle you want to live up to. The only thing you will gain from him is respect, and that's one the most important factors you need going into any relationship. PESKY girls set rules for themselves, and in turn are princesses to all the boys they meet.

List all the lovey-dovey nicknames you have given your beaus:

_____

List all the cutesy-tootsy nicknames beaus have given you:

_____

Place a photo of your #1 amour here

It's Real PESKY LOVE When You . . .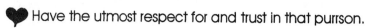

♥ Have the utmost respect for and trust in that purrson.

♥ Feel comfee communicating with about your deepest & most honest thoughts.

♥ Are able to balance the time you spend with him and time you spend with your friends and family, and he knows to do the same.

♥ Have in no way compromised who you are inside to make him like you better.

♥ Enjoy that you don't have everything in common. Opposites really *do* attract.

My Current Crushes:

♡ Randolph Sellers—My one & only geek love!
♡ John Cusack—Please . . . *Say Anything* to me!
♡ Peter Sellers—His flicks rock my projector.
♡ Andrew McCarthy—"Pretty in Pout."
♡ John, Ringo, George, & Paul—"The Bee-ulls."
♡ Abraham Lincoln—He's the Victorian era's Elvis!
♡ Harold Lloyd—The cute king of silent film comedy.

Songs for Falling in Crush To:

Crazy for You—Madonna
God Only Knows—The Beach Boys
I Will—The Beatles
Hopelessly Devoted To You—Olivia Newton-John
You Look So Fine—Garbage
Anything by The Supremes
I Will Always Love You—Dolly Parton
Lost In Your Eyes—Debbie Gibson
True—Spandau Ballet
My Secret Love—Doris Day

List tunes that have rocked your romantic world:

_____

_____

_____

Who was your first mondo-crush?

_____

I'm Lucky in Love!

List all your current subjects of swoon:

_____

_____

_____

_____

_____

_____

_____

_____

_____

_____

_____

The Essential Ingredients for a Truly Pesky Peck are . . .

- A cute, sweet, well-groomed boy.

- The strongest mints you can find.

- Yummy flavored lip gloss (The ones i'm diggin' the most are Bonne Bell's Lip Smacker in Razzleberry, Bloom's vanilla, and Rachel Perry's banana/coconut. Warning: Usage of any of the above may cause him to devour you.

- An Angora sweater and bullet bra (Every '50s pin-up girl needs her ammunition!)

- A boom box playing kissy tunes.

Which flirting techniques do you find to be the most fun?

_____

_____

Tips for Smoochin':

Do it like they do in black-&-white movies . . . Don't practice on melons or anything, just let it happen naturally and romantically. Keep it rated PG (Pesky Girl!) until you are over eighteen, then YOU decide when to give him the green light to go any further. I am so sick of the media shoving all this sex malarkey in our faces, making you feel like a freak if you haven't "done it" yet. Don't pay any attention! You have my permission to live like Sandra Dee or Jane Austen's Emma. Be a lil' Miss Goody Prude Shoes!

The Big Love Scene

Give me all the juicy details of your first kiss ♥

Who? _____

What? _____

Where? _____

When? _____

Here you can make a list of all the boys you've kissed ♥

_____

_____

_____

_____

_____

_____

_____

I just hope I gave you enough room!

L'AMOUR,   L'AMOUR

I Know I'm Crazy in Crush When . . .

♥ I have the insatiable urge to bake heart-shaped gooey cookies.

♥ I make him a 90-min. compilation tape of my fave songs.

♥ I bring my tight white bad-girl sweater to the dry cleaners.

♥ No boys at the Pavement concert are even remotely cute.

♥ Every romantic comedy I watch reminds me of us.

♥ I actually care if his parents dig me.

♥ I don't mind taking hour-long trips with him to Home Depot.

♥ I wear no makeup in front of him so he can see the real me.

What are the signs that you're crazy In Crush?

_____

_____

_____

_____

_____

_____

What's the craziest thing you've done to grab a hottie's attention?

_____

_____

_____

_____

_____

♥ Something to Remember: ♥

Boys worry about how they look just as much as you do, and are just as insecure about approaching you as you would be in approaching them.

Maintaining Pesky-ness on the First Date . . . Wardrobe-Wise!

Unless you live in Death Valley, and it's 110 degrees outside . . . please say no to the micro-mini, platforms, and tube top date ensemb. Wearing an outfit that is trying *too* hard to be sexy for your crush is just too obvious, and may even give him a sign that you are insecure. Your object of hottie-ness wants to feel 100% comfee around you, respect you, and know you are the kind of girl who can throw on a pair of Levi's, a worn-out sweater, and zero makeup for an eve of cuddling while viewing *The Matrix*. (Just for the record, I've just described every boy's dream date!)

While boys may seem floored at your keen ability to out-babe Pamela Anderson Lee . . . it also makes your boy a tad nervous. He might think, "Does she always dress this provocatively? Does this mean she's high-maintenance?" And it also puts pressure on him to take you somewhere "hot & happenin" . . . like you're gonna be disappointed if you're not taken someplace worthy of your attire. I mean, when you're wearing stilettos and a noir dress featuring a sky-high slit up the side . . . his plans for taking you miniature golfing will surely be squashed. So be considerate of him in your date garb, because he'd find you sexy in a potato sack (but at least apply blush if you're gonna go *that* route).

What NOT to Wear:

Miniskirts resembling Band-Aids—You'll send him the wrong message. Old-fashioned? Yes . . . but many boys are totally self-control retarded. But if you really feel that your gams are your bod's best asset, at least invest in a karate course before putting them on display.

Peek-a-boob! . . . It's a tube top—It's not the swingin' '70s, and I really doubt he's taking you to boogie at Studio 54, so please don't go for the ultra-obvious "Hey, big boy, check my melons" look. To even an eighteen-year-old boy . . . that is just plain cruel.

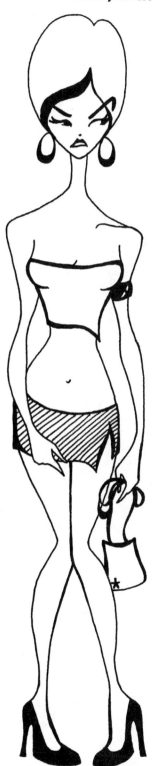

Stolen stilettos from Mommy—The cute boys I know think that Frederick's-style ho-heels look lame on girls under thirty. Try wearing ballet slippers, Mary Janes, or Beatle boots instead. Boys dream of kissing innocents like Liv Tyler or Audrey Hepburn (both lovers of flat shoes) . . . Otherwise you will just be contributing to increases in Dr. Scholl's stock value. It's much more feminine to be able to run along the beach, dance painlessly, or go on a long after-movie stroll than to look like a fourteen-year-old dressed as a porn star for Halloween.

So much makeup that you pray for a dark destination—Here is something that I swear on my cat Tallulah's life . . . Boys hate being able to *see* that you are wearing makeup. And I hate to be the one to break it to you, but, YES, they can see your zits! Here's the good news . . . They don't give a hoot about about your pimples *or* if your lip liner is straight. Actually, they'd much prefer it if you'd remove it altogether so that it won't get all over their mug when they go in for a smooch. Go easy on the greasepaint. Concentrate on having confidence, and to him your blemishes will become beauty marks.

DO Bring the following Pesky Accoutrements:

A SWEATER—I know the score . . . It's 10 below freezing, but you "forgot" to bring a sweater because you knew it would mess up that perfect view of your décolletage in that new Wonderbra. Unless it's fun trying to convince him that "Shivering Blue Lips" is Chanel's latest shade, as well as making him freeze 'cuz he insisted you take his coat . . . veto the boobie top, and pop on a tight fuzzy '50s pin-up girl sweater instead. It's much smarter, sexier, and you won't have pneumonia the next day.

SOME "MAD MONEY"—Just in case he makes you steamin' MAD and you have to call a cab, or if he doesn't offer to pay for anything (which would kill his chances of ever seeing moi again). $10 to $20 will suffice (depending on whether you get mad before or after you buy your own movie ticket).

FLAVORED lip gloss—But try to use this only after the first date . . . if you catch my drift.

Leave Every Date With a Happy Ending:
Double-date until you feel you trust him.

Take a self-defense class. Watch all three Karate Kid movies beforehand. This way, if he gets too fresh, you'll be pumped when it comes time to kick boy butt.

Make him STOP! LOOK! and LOVE! ♥

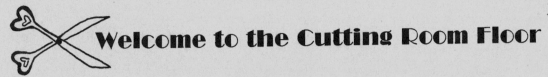

Welcome to the Cutting Room Floor

Don't Cast the Following NON-Pesky Boys in Your Flick . . . They Are the Ones Who . . .

★ Aren't good listeners and only want to talk about themselves.

★ Smoke cigarettes (it's like kissing an ashtray, echhh!)

★ Aren't groomed properly. Most boys *do* need help from us squeaky-clean girls in this dept. Remember the age-old saying . . . Girls="sugar & spice & everything nice . . ." Boys="snakes & snails & puppy dog tails . . ."

★ Aren't supportive of every dream you're trying to fulfill.

★ Always take your date money when you offer to pay.

★ Kiss other girls (or do more than that. Yuck!)

★ Are jealous of the time you spend with your friends.

★ Say things hurtful to your self-esteem, or have ever physically hurt you. Dump these un-Pesky boys ASAP!

List all your signs that a boy is NON-Pesky material: _____

_____

_____

When on a Date with a Boy . . . NEVER Have the Following Conversation . . .

Him: What do you wanna do tonight?
You: Whatever you wanna do.
Him: Oh, I don't care. I'll leave it up to you.
You: It really doesn't matter to me, anything is good.
Him: Yeah, I don't care either . . . do you?
You: I'll just do whatever you wanna do . . .

Sound familiar? This is that typical lame first-date conversation about where to go, and it can be avoided by simply thinking of some options before your beau arrives. Instead of looking like some opinionless servant to the male species, just suggest *anything*! I promise you this . . . He really doesn't care where you go, especially if *he* asked *you* out. He just wants to be graced with your supreme presence. And if you start out his night of intrigue by having no opinions at all, you'll only destroy his dream of a confident and creative girl. So don't make it too hard on the poor worshipful boy . . . suggest a bad flick, a swing set in the park, Pictionary, anything! Just make it Pesky, like you!

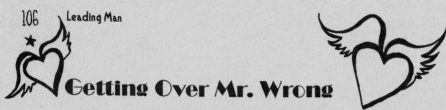

Getting Over Mr. Wrong

There are good things you can get out of having had a Poopy ex-boy. You need not dwell on what you may have done wrong, what was wrong with him, or, worst option yet . . . how you can get back together. I firmly believe . . . and this is out of much experience, darlin' . . . that once you've given or received ye old heave-ho, there should be no goin' back. Once it's over . . . it's over. Going back into any past relationship is like regressing in life. It's like saying that you don't deserve anyone better, and that's just not true. It's much healthier to move on, and mentally reminisce about the good or bad times you once had . . . but never actually relive the relationship.

Another thing you should *never* do, is "regret" having been with anyone, no matter what a huge "mistake" you think your relationship was. Maybe you are humiliated because you acted a certain way while you were with him that led your friends to think you were lame, or you feel you went a little too far physically with your ex, and you regret it . . . Well, just remember that you should . . . to quote Madonna from "Human Nature," have "absolutely no regrets." There are no mistakes in life . . . Everything happens for a reason, and the worst thing you could get from any Poopy ex-relationship is actually something awesome . . . it's *experience*. If you learned one single thing that will assist you for the rest of your life in making better decisions, then wasn't knowing that bad-boy worth it? Stand by all the decisions you've made, past and future, because in the end it will only make you a more mature girl . . . with a keen relationship sense to guide her on the journey to finding her purrfect Pesky soul mate.

WHEN *Cupid* SENDS YOU THAT SPARKLY NEW BOY, DON'T DISS YOUR FRIENDS.

There is one annoying thing that has gone on since the beginning of time, and most girls still haven't learned . . . It is the following . . . When you fall into the hole of infatuation with your new beau . . . don' t think your girl friends won't notice that you are completely ditching them. We all know how this works . . . Your best friend inevitably gets jealous of all the quality time you're spending with your boy toy, and not her, especially if you invite her along to the movies as that all-humiliating "third wheel," and her bonus prize is that used feeling she gets the minute something goes awry in loveland . . . and you glom on to her like she's Dr. Drew giving free love advice in the mall. Don't let this happen to you. Be mature about it, or you very well might end up a lonely girl when your friend gets fed up and her shoulder to cry on becomes too tired to hold your head.

Try to schedule enough time for both of them. Set aside a movie date one night on the weekend for just you & her, or go shopping on Saturdays, get pedicures together, go for a milkshake, check out cute boys, anything! . . . just don't neglect her, and then she won't do the same to you when she's seriously smitten. There is another upside to spending time away from your man . . . He'll dig you more! He'll think it's healthy and girly that you need time away from him to do your own thang. He'll respect that you have your own life and you don't need to observe his every movement. Boys can feel stifled by girls easily, and they especially dig girls who are secure enough in theirselves to trust him to have his time with *his* friends too. One of the quickest ways to screw up a relationship is to act like he *is* your life . . . ignoring all your previous obligations, friends, family, and hobbies. That just builds a doomed relationship from the get-go. And one more thing . . . Finding a beau who is also your best friend is fine . . . Don't cheat yourself out of other potentially blooming relationships.

Signs You Are in a Poopy Relationship:

♥ Thoughts like "Things will get better *one day*" always run through your mind.

♥ You're constantly asking if he loves you, and are in need of daily reassurance.

♥ You don't trust him to be alone with his girl "friends."

♥ You don't feel comfee being yourself around him, and alter your purrsonality according to what you think he'll dig.

The Climactic Breakup Scene: ✱

Look through old photos of happier times, *cry a lot* , then move on! The last thing you want to do is overreact . . . like this boy in the '80s I read about who rode his bike off a cliff after hearing that *Battlestar Galactica* was canceled. There is no time for dwelling on the painful past. You've got way too much yummy stuff in your future. I know how much it hurts to have your heart smushed, it feels like you'll never find anyone else like him, or as good as him again . . . right? Well, WRONG . . . You'll find someone even better!

Please don't torture your lovely friends and families with all the minuscule details of your breakup. Don't bore them with endless analyzations of what went wrong . . . Just sum up what you think went sour in 100 words or less and write the rest in your diary. Then, when you've said everything in your heart that hurts . . . put the diary in a locked-up box at the back of your closet . . . bury it in the backyard or place it in the storage shed, along with all the old photos of him . . . any place you can visit him later in life if you feel the need.

After you've used up all the Kleenex in the house . . . move on! Think of it this way . . . If your arms are occupied clutching past memories and burning torches for the ex-guy . . . there is no room for them to hold that new fab boy out there looking for a girl just like you. You've got to make room for someone more deserving of your Pesky-ness. There will always be that memory box in the back storage shelves of your heart, and you can open it up anytime to remember that stinky-ex. Breaking up is good for one thing . . . You can apply lessons you've learned to help assist you in getting through new dramas unscathed. Just stop thinking any of those supernegative thoughts about never finding love again, blah, blah . . . do some healthy boudoir redecorating in that huge luxurious room that is your heart . . . and have a garage sale . . . You'll need all that emotional room for new fun, creativity, and the next hottie that comes your way.

Runny Mascara . . . Music for Breaking Up To:

C'mon, get it all out . . . let the tears flow and the tunes blast. I will now suggest to you some of *the* saddest CDs to torture your weeping ears with post-heartbreak. After all, us damsels need a good hard cry every once in a while in times of distress, it's healthy. Get him and all the hurt out of your system by torturing yourself with these empowering yet bittersweet ballads. I find myself turning on the waterworks about once a week, and it rejuvenates me. And after you've wept over all the tragically brilliant lyrics of young love lost, you'll then be a stronger girl . . . ready to reface your public, and ready to fall in crush with a new specimen of swankiness all over again. So pull a Garbo on your parents by exclaiming her signature statement . . . "I vannnt to be aloone!" . . . and get those pink tissues ready for some tunes to clear your tear ducts out completely. Boo-hoo, sniff sniff . . .

For When Your Heart's Been Broken Into Tiny Pink Pieces . . .

I'm Gonna Be Strong—Cyndi Lauper
Without Your Love—Billie Holiday
Cry Me a River—Julie London
Goodbye to Romance—Ozzy Osbourne
Last Night I Dreamt That Somebody Loved Me—The Smiths
I Fall to Pieces and Crazy—Patsy Cline
Forever Blue—Chris Isaak
Blue Days, Black Nights—Buddy Holly
Live Through This—Hole
Ex-Girlfriend—No Doubt
Barracuda—Heart
Love Is a Battlefield and Heartbreaker—Pat Benatar
As Tears Go By—Marianne Faithfull
Bye Bye Love—The Cars

When was the last time you had a long cry, and what prompted you? _____

_____

_____

_____

To all the very UN-Pesky boys in the world we say . . .
Don't call us . . . we'll call you.

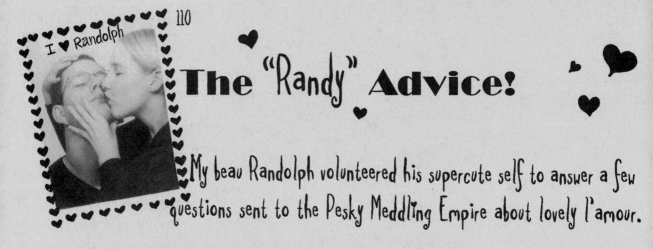

I ♥ Randolph

110

The "Randy" Advice!

My beau Randolph volunteered his supercute self to answer a few questions sent to the Pesky Meddling Empire about lovely l'amour.

Does a boy prefer a girl to play hard to get, or should she just call him? Also, do boys like a girl with a pierced nose? *Meghan, 15*

I was always too stupid to tell "hard to get" from "not at all interested in you whatsoever," so I'd say don't play it *too* cool. But no one, boy or girl, wants to be pursued by someone who is needy or desperate. So, if you feel like you'll explode if he isn't your boyfriend by next Tuesday, then hang up the phone. But there's nothing wrong with calling up a boy and asking him out for some non-threatening fun. Maybe he wants to ask you out but doesn't have the nerve? He'll appreciate the chance to hang out in a non-date way, and will probably take it from there. As for nose rings, some boys like them, some don't, and some don't care. Don't poke a hole in yourself because some boy you haven't met yet might like it. A smart boy will see through you if you only do it because you think it's cool or whatever. If you want the ring because you feel like a pierced-nose chick who is missing a hole, go for it. Otherwise, don't.

The boy I have a crush on at school treats me like the plague . . . I know we share similar interests (music, films, etc.), but I can't seem to get his attention. What should I do? *Molly, 13*

I once liked a girl at school so much that I hit her in the head with an apple. So, I think this boy has a crush on you too. He is treating you like a disease because his crush makes him feel like he has one. He wants to talk to you, but he doesn't know how. Here is your mission: You have to do his job for him and ask him out. Figure out a way to talk to him alone, so that he won't feel any pressure from his friends to act cool. Since you have similar tastes, ask him to go see a movie that you think he would like. This way, you're more likely to become the apple of his eye than to get one in your eye.

Why do boys always like the bad girls at school? The ones who smoke and dress sleazy? *Leigha, 19*

You can't underestimate the power of advertising, but you can always offer a superior product. To the boys, these chicks look like the shortcut to Sin City, but the last thing you want to do is to trash up your look and start puffing on a Marlboro just to snag some mindless boyfriend. Instead, show classy style of your own, and the right boy will pop up.

I like hanging out with this cute stoner boy at school, but he always asks me if I want to smoke pot, and I'm just not into it. How do I make him understand that I want to be with him, not his bong? *Melanie, 19*

A bong can give a boy a sense of self-confidence, cool, and personality, for about an hour, that is, until he needs his plastic friend to give him another blast. I think your boy feels inadequate and guilty, and he wants you to join him so he'll feel like it's okay for him to be stoned. Tell him you aren't going to smoke, but you want to hang out because you like him, especially when he's not baked. Eventually, he'll get the idea and stop hiding behind a cloud. Some advice for the future: Stoners get dull in the long term, because you can't develop as a person when you're high. He'll have to cut way back, or you'll have to move on.

My boyfriend and I have been seeing each other for two years. Lately, the spark just doesn't seem to be there. I'm a pretty girl, so I get asked out often. Recently, an old guy friend that I have always been crushin' on asked me out. Do you think I'm a bad girl if I go? *Cupcake, 18*

Cheating is a two-way street, and although you say the spark is out, how would you feel if your boyfriend went on a date without telling you? You've invested two years with your boy, so it's probably worth the effort to be honest with him. If you've known the new boy awhile, I assume he knows you have a boyfriend. If so, what is he doing asking you out? Either he's rude and unworthy of you, or you're putting out a serious "available" vibe. Whichever, you need to make a decision about "Old Faithful" at home, and pick one or none of these boys soon.

I have a crush on my best boy-friend (a Duckie!). How do I tell him without ruining our friendship? *Lizzie, 21*

Not telling him can ruin everything as easily as telling him. Your crush will affect the way you act around him, and you can't hide it forever. I think the best romances are just friendships with some snogging blended in, and you're already halfway there. You have a big advantage over most couples because you already *know* you like each other. Just look at it as adding another layer to the friendship you already have. It might not work out, but you have to at least give it a shot.

What signals to a boy that a girl is insecure? *Jennifur, 24*

Girls that are dressing way too sexy for their age are actually insecure. Or, wearing exactly what everyone else is wearing can also make you appear insecure.

How fab is this boy action?

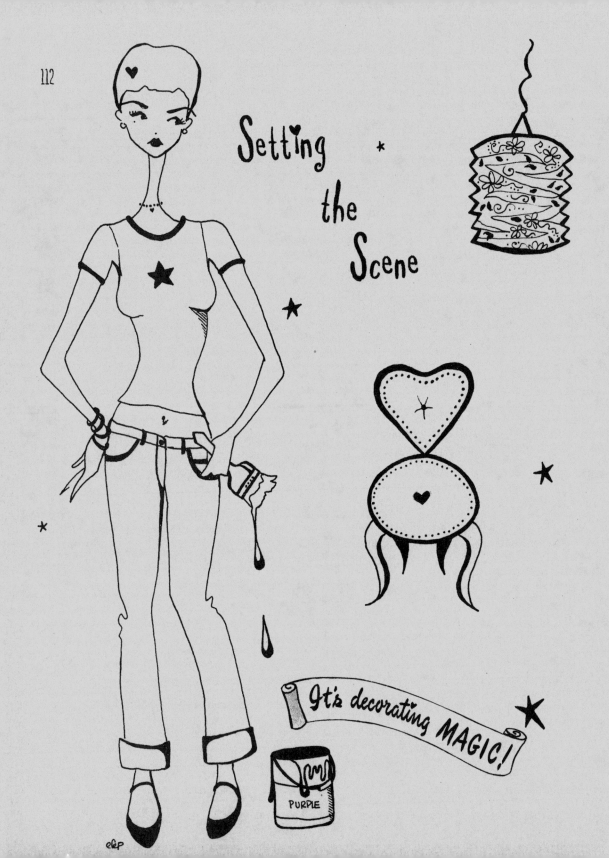

Setting the Scene

It's decorating MAGIC!

PURPLE

Setting the Scene

"Home is anywhere I hang my wig."—Dolly Parton

Your bedroom is in no way just a "room" . . . it is your purrsonal sanctuary, your temple, your mini Taj Mahal, your private movie palace. The space in which you live should never be neglected, because it is a reflection of who you are. It's like a comfee cocoon for all your thoughts and ideas to bloom within. So let's now figure out how to set the stage for the star that is you.

Pretend You Are a Set Designer . . .
Let's Decorate Your Boudoir to Fit Your Purrsonality !

The key to having a warm and stylish living space is to fill it only with things that you really cherish, love, and adore.

Don't live like Oscar the Grouch! Pizza crusts under the bed, glasses of juice fermenting on your dresser. Creating a garbage-filled environment for yourself will only make your self esteem feel like garbage. You are not a college football player, so tidy, tidy, girls!

If you feel unhappy when hanging out in your room, chances are you need to let in a little more light. A brighter environment makes for a brighter outlook. I used to feel melancholy while spending time in my boudoir, and then I figured out that my room gets hardly any sunlight, making the vibe seem dreary. I added some happy lamps , and voilà! Euphoric ambience!

If you usually feel too hyper to go to sleep on time, chances are you have the opposite problem, too much light. If you need to chill, do as the Donna Summer disco song says . . . "Dim all the lights, sweet darlin'." Or try hanging some deep colored Indian fabrics on your walls as tapestries. cozy colors equal sleepytime.

List your fave items currently decorating your "set," and where you found them:

_____

_____

_____

SET DECOR FOR YOUR PESKY BOUDOIR

Having a messy room sucks! I know this because in high school I decided that dirty velvet vintage dresses and old cups of lichen-growing cranberry juice were appropriate forms of decor. I was (Big Surprise!) depressed. I couldn't concentrate on homework or art projects and felt poopy about myself. Let's be honest . . . When you haven't picked your clothes up off the floor for a least a week and under your bed lives a peanut butter & jelly sandwich that could win first place at the next science fair, how can you feel clearheaded and enthused? Now that I have altered my set decor, I am the polar opposite of that dirty, depressed, high school baby . . . I love my tiny boudoir. It is my sanctuary of all that is art deco and girly. My room went from being a rave-flyer-infested pigsty to a Pesky palace . . . a true reflection of me!

When it comes to decorating, you don't need a lot of cash to do something fab. If it's cooler furniture you need, try a thrift shop, flea market, or my purrsonal fave . . . Grandma's storage shed. With any ol' brown '70s chair or wood coffee table, the possibilities are endless. When strategizing how you are going to give your place a makeover, try and visualize your dream decor. If it's anything like a decorating dream of mine, then chances are it will be tacky. Reaching tacky-ness is always a great aesthetic goal, 'cuz it's really easy to achieve.

Here are some Pesky art supplies to stock up on . . . you'll never run out of uses for them:

❄ A small hot-glue gun and glue sticks. (Be careful! I've burned myself many times with my beloved one.)

❄ Metallic spray paint—perfect to give thrift-store furniture a groovy new look. I'm never without gold. (You should spray outside, wear a painter's mask, and put down tons of newspaper. Don't ruin your parents' driveway . . . like I did.)

❄ Big jars of your fave color glitter. (You can use it as makeup too.)

❄ A couple yards of Day-Glo fun-fur or faux leopard fur. Great for sewing crazy throw pillows by hand, the more awkward and homemade looking, the better! You can also upholster chairs with it, or line the inside of a collaged knickknack box. To do fun & easy reupholstery, use a staple gun, which always makes me feel powerful like the Bionic Woman. (Another warning from Miss Caution: Aim carefully at the furniture in question so you don't shoot your pretty eye out!)

Just use your imagination, it's endless . . . the adorable damage one can do! Decide what kind of image you want to portray to visitors . . . Is it '40s Vargas pin-up queen? . . . For this I would do a pink marabou feather phone, Rit-dye a chenille bedspread pink, baby blue, or violet.

Or do you want to live like a '20s silent screen goddess/art deco revivalist? This is the look I'm currently trying to emulate . . . It's all about ornate velvet throw pillows and a vintage burgundy satin duvet cover, silent film posters and worn-out tapestry rugs, green velvet theater curtains . . . It's fit for Clara Bow . . . and moi too!

Of course, how about a burlesque showgirls' saloon dressing room circa the old West, like Marlene Dietrich had in *The Seven Sinners* ? Then there's the supercool pad of a '60s mod-ster . . . all white with a black-&- white checkered floor and a space-age bubble record player with a huge op-art poster from the flick *Blow-up* adorning the wall . . . and not to forget the rockin' '80s, where you'd have tons fluorescent stuff strewn everywhere . . . Go-Go's albums, a jewelry box overflowing with new wave band pins, a poster from *The Breakfast Club*, and a splatter-painted coffee table to scatter your jelly bracelets upon . . .

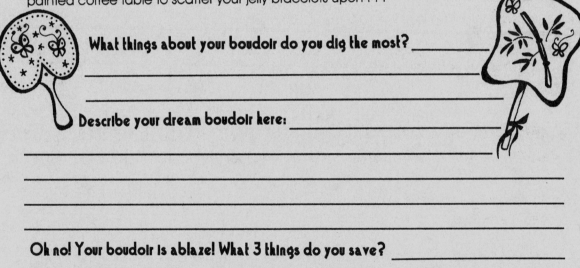

What things about your boudoir do you dig the most? _____
_____
_____

Describe your dream boudoir here: _____
_____
_____
_____
_____

Oh no! Your boudoir is ablaze! What 3 things do you save? _____
_____
_____

★ **Me in homage to the cover of Cyndi Lauper's classic '80s album *She's So Unusual*.** ★

Choosing Your Soundtrack

Your theme song should be your ultimate inspirational tune—the song you'd love to blast on level 10 of your boom box as you get dressed everyday. It should be a representation of who you are at the moment. The lyrics are so about you that you'd swear the songwriter used you as their unbeknownst muse. Or maybe the tune just rocks. It should be iconic . . . like in the beginning of *Saturday Night Fever* when you see only John Travolta's pimp booties walkin' down the street to the pulse of The BeeGees' "Stayin' Alive." It set the tone for the entire film . . . and the song presented perfectly the essence of his character . . . and an entire era. Or in the opening credits of *Pretty in Pink* where Molly Ringwald is in her house on the wrong side of the tracks putting together her flowery vintage ensemble and glossing her legendary pout to the Psychedic Furs tune "Pretty in Pink."

Rising out of your bed in the morning cues your opening credits . . . What better way to start them rolling than with a press of the play button to start your purrsonal Pesky compilation tape? And even if you don't own a bitchin' stereo to play your tunes on, you always have the pink boom box in your mind . . . (Mine is constantly playing different girly theme songs as I strut my stuff through the city. It's always inspiring to know that the power of Madonna is always with me . . . stereo or not.)

What is your theme song? _____

Which song has affected you the most deeply? _____

What was the first record you ever bought? _____

What is your fave Beatles tune? _____

"Don't stand in the corner, waitin' for a chance . . . make your own music, start your own dance"

—Madonna from "Spotlight"

Achieving True RECORD NERD Status...
and Yes... that's a good thing.

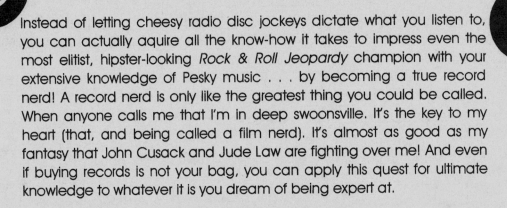

Instead of letting cheesy radio disc jockeys dictate what you listen to, you can actually aquire all the know-how it takes to impress even the most elitist, hipster-looking *Rock & Roll Jeopardy* champion with your extensive knowledge of Pesky music . . . by becoming a true record nerd! A record nerd is only like the greatest thing you could be called. When anyone calls me that I'm in deep swoonsville. It's the key to my heart (that, and being called a film nerd). It's almost as good as my fantasy that John Cusack and Jude Law are fighting over me! And even if buying records is not your bag, you can apply this quest for ultimate knowledge to whatever it is you dream of being expert at.

A true record nerd needs not know every single thing about the history of music. In fact, they usually know diddly about opera or New Age (yuck!), but they are like musical scavengers. Everything they find leading to another piece of information, and more killer tunes.

To a record nerd, the history of music is like a giant tree . . . you should climb many branches in order to find what may be your style of leaf. The first step to *really* knowing what you're listening to is by reading the liner notes on an album (just like you should read the credits following any film you love). Chances are that two tunes you dig were written by the same person, or recorded by the same producer. . . Pretend your new fave song is "Fever" by Madonna from the album *Erotica* . . . What a record nerd would do next is to read the credits of and see who wrote it. The purrson who wrote it is Peggy Lee, so you'd go and buy Peggy's greatest hits. You then say, YOWZA!, her version of "Fever" is even swankier than Maddy's because it's so sultry & loungy! If you then become obsessed with finding more versions of the tune, you can do more research, look on the Internet, and come up with dozens of versions (some great, some stinky) of your new fave song. (The Cramps do a fun surf-rock version of "Fever" as well.)

Usually only boys are referred to as record nerds, which makes it even better for us girls because we are a rare find, and the guys know that. It's kind of like showing a boy that you can race cars. They will drool over your ability to scare any MTV VJ with your vast knowledge of all that has been rotated on a turntable at any point in history. Boys are always smittenly impressed when they think they're saying something that will go over my pretty head, and I hit them with a wallop of info about the subject. In fact, I had a boy lecturing his pals in front of me once, saying things like . . . "Every girl's CD collection sucks," and "Girls usually only have only one cool CD, and that's because their boyfriend bought it for them." . . . Screw that noise! Let's show 'em!

Finding links and connections from one record to another will create a more varied CD collection and will lead you to finding new things you'll love that radio and your friends may never expose you to . . . It's like the difference between being the drummer for the band, and being the drummer's girlfriend.

Even if you find only one tune you adore by following my suggestions . . . then my job is done. And like a Pesky pied piper, you'll find your own flute, and you too will become a guru of sound for other Pesky girls to follow until they "diskover" their record nerd within. So now, my lil' rock & rollers . . . I want you to go practice the three R's of becoming a true record nerdette . . . **Review, Research, and Rock!**

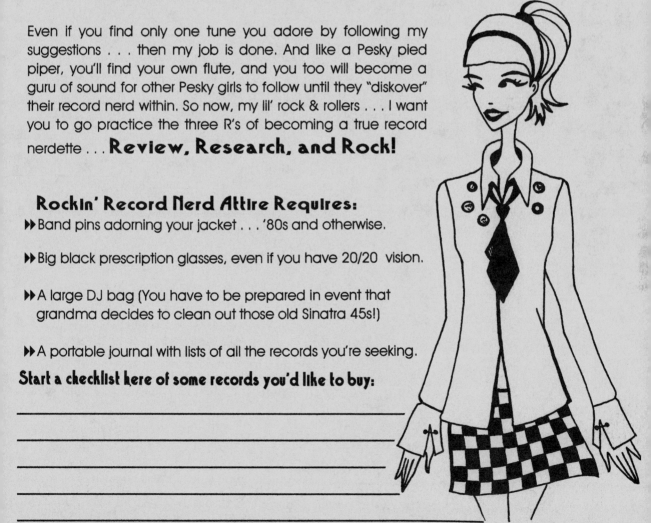

Rockin' Record Nerd Attire Requires:

▶▶ Band pins adorning your jacket . . . '80s and otherwise.

▶▶ Big black prescription glasses, even if you have 20/20 vision.

▶▶ A large DJ bag (You have to be prepared in event that grandma decides to clean out those old Sinatra 45s!)

▶▶ A portable journal with lists of all the records you're seeking.

Start a checklist here of some records you'd like to buy:

_____

_____

_____

_____

ekp

Scoring Your Film

Every Pesky girl's life should be filled to the brim with music. Hearing a tune we love can make us feel happy, make us weepy, trigger fond memories, make us do the Twist, and turn an otherwise boring day into one filled with neon disco-glitter rainbows. Without music I would be one melancholy kitten. There's no way for me to even reminisce about my childhood without remembering all the hundreds of Saturday morning lip-synching pajama parties I had with my friends. We would sneak into my mom's closet and swipe her feather boa, gold high heels, smear red lipstick all over our lips, and do our best impersonations of Madonna rolling all over the floor in the "Like a Virgin" video. What you and I are now going to do is explore all different kinds of Pesky music and create the soundtrack for your life.

What is Pesky music, you ask? Well, for moi . . . Pesky music is anything that inspires me to create, get down on the dance floor, (and do lip- synch routines whilst standing on my bed). It should be performed by an artist I consider to be a Pesky purrson, and it should add a cinematic vibe to my life when I press the play button.

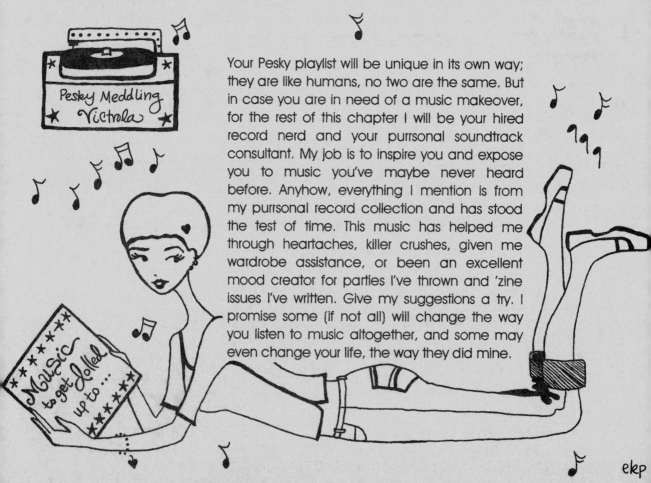

Your Pesky playlist will be unique in its own way; they are like humans, no two are the same. But in case you are in need of a music makeover, for the rest of this chapter I will be your hired record nerd and your purrsonal soundtrack consultant. My job is to inspire you and expose you to music you've maybe never heard before. Anyhow, everything I mention is from my purrsonal record collection and has stood the test of time. This music has helped me through heartaches, killer crushes, given me wardrobe assistance, or been an excellent mood creator for parties I've thrown and 'zine issues I've written. Give my suggestions a try. I promise some (if not all) will change the way you listen to music altogether, and some may even change your life, the way they did mine.

ekp

Here are my current Pesky soundtrack picks:

Xanadu (soundtrack)—Olivia Newton-John & ELO

Rubber Soul—The Beatles

Paper Moon (SOUNDTRACK)

Let Me Entertain You—Ann-Margret

Blade Runner (soundtrack)—Vangelis

Black Sabbath—Black Sabbath

Pink Moon—Nick Drake

Rich Kid Blues—Marianne Faithfull

List your current soundtrack picks:

_____

_____

_____

_____

_____

If you had a band what would you name it? _____

Design your first CD cover here:

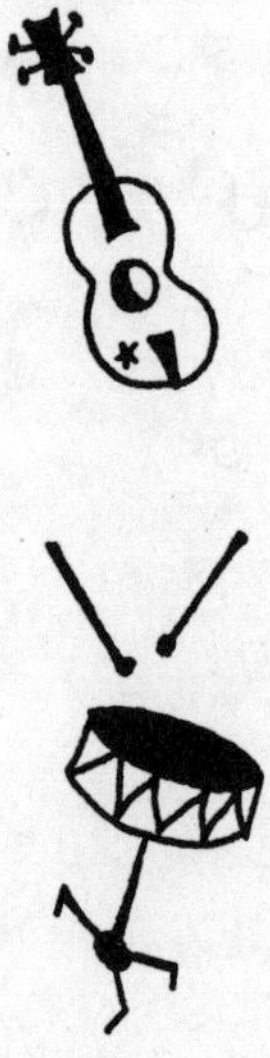

Rockin' Pesky
Thing To Do:

If you have trouble waking up early, like moi . . . try starting your day with a high-energy lip-sync performance of your fave tune. Jump on your bed, use a brush as a microphone, try on potential ensembs, have fun!

Cyndi Lauper... *my fave Pesky rocker!*

I was eight years old when I first discovered the legendary Miss Lauper. I had entered a community talent show with some other Lauper-wanna-bees . . . The song we lip-sanc to was later to become my Pesky anthem . . . "Girls Just Wanna Have Fun." She's a punk rock flapper from Brooklyn, with the voice of a Blue Angel (the name of her very first band), not to mention being a true Renaissance girl (fab actress, music video director, mother, even designs her own tour tees!), and she was wearing vintage bustiers and petticoats while Madonna was still in Huggies.

The first time I had my eyes blessed by her presence in person, was her Hat Full of Stars Tour and she just floored me. When she sang "Change of Heart," the crowd just went berzerk! Cyndi asked all her security guards to leave, jumped offstage, and started dancing with my friends and I! She then hugged and kissed me on the cheek, and we did the Ringwald (a cute '80s dance Molly does in *The Breakfast Club*). They wrote about *my* Cyndi encounter in the L.A. *Times* the next day, describing me as a "worshipful fan."

I now refer to her simply as "The Voice," and you can't deny the fact that there's no one like her. If you aren't awestruck by her already, then please give her a chance to prove to you that she's more than just some product of the '80s. To me she's her royal highness of vintage Vaudeville. Words cannot express how much I WORSHIP this epitome of a Pesky girl! (I guess the L.A. *Times was* right in their description of moi). She'll bop in my heart always!

Cyndi drawings by Jennifer   photos: Kevin Dornan

"Some boys take a beautiful girl, and hide her away from the rest of the world . . . I want to be the one to walk in the sun. Oh girls! . . . they want to have fun!"

—Cyndi Lauper

Who is your fave Pesky rocker?

_____

When dressing in homage to Cyndi . . . try some of these:

Cyndi

- ♥ All the sparkly, tacky, rhinestone jewelry you can find
- ★ Fluorescent Halloween hair spray and a crimping iron
- ♥ Fishnets layered over colored tights
- ★ Combat boots or '50s kitten heels
- ♥ Vintage bustiers customized with rhinestones, pins, feathers, and anything fun you can think of!
- ★ A hair bow made of crinoline
- ★ Shapes made with eye shadow on your lids (hearts, stars, swirls, etc . . .)
- ♥ A tiara paired with your fave old pair of jeans
- ★ Plastic bangles covering your entire forearm
- ♥ Poufy prom dresses with wacky belts
- ★ Bowling shirts with '50s girl names on them like Ethel
- ♥ A faux leopard coat adorned with '80s band pins

It's me again!

Dressed as the goddess Cyndi.

Cyndi albums you should get:
- ★ SHE'S SO UNUSUAL (a Pesky classic!)
- ★ BLUE ANGEL (Her very first! When she was only a teen!)
- ★ TWELVE DEADLY CYNS . . . (Her 'best of' compilation)

moi as cyndi

Cyndi in the 1980's

Girls Just Want To Have Fun written by Robert Hazard

Here I am, singing "Hooray for Hollywood!"

On Location

IT'S TRAVEL TIME!

Traveling doesn't have to be about flying on United Airlines someplace exotic. Traveling can simply be about walking down the street from your house, just as long as you are creative about it and make the trip into an adventure. Due to lack of funds and a busy schedule . . . I, purrsonally, have never even been out of the U.S. (Even though I plan on becoming a European jet-setter soon. We should all shoot for the sky, kitties!) But one thing I have done is explored my city to it's fullest. So when a friend visits me from another state and says, "Show me around" . . . I can take them on a trip to paint the town pink, like no Universal Studios tour guide ever could. Hollywood and I have always had a love/hate relationship (LOVE: the old architecture & movie palace; HATE: the smog & traffic), but love conquers all, so I made it my mission to get to know the city I was born & raised in on a first-name basis . . . and I think you should try the same. Become, as they are known in the biz, a LOCATION SCOUT. Instead of being bored with seeing the same stuff out the car window every day, or hanging out in the same mall . . . EXPLORE where you live, and you'll find Pesky beauty you never knew existed there.

PESKY THINGS TO DO:

✈ Buy a book on cool old architecture and go around your town trying to figure out what style of design each intriguing house or building is.

✈ If there are any museums you've never been to near your house, grab a date or go solo, just go! You may see something that will change the way you look at life.

✈ Take a daytime road trip with your friends. It doesn't matter where you go . . . Sunbathe in a field, go roller-skating, have a picnic, buy disposable cameras and take photos of whatever you find inspiring, or just drive around and sing along to tunes on the radio . . . it's just so cathartic to get out of town for even one day. (No automobile? Just live by the immortal words of Nancy Sinatra . . . "These boots are made for walkin'.")

List all the beautiful things about where you live: _____

_____

List the places in your town that you've always wanted to enter, but never have:

_____

le bon voyage

The following is a list of lil' Pesky things I've learned during my past travels of the good ol' U.S.A. For this section I would have loved to have done research in Paris, but my Pesky piggy bank couldn't cover it . . . C'est la vie! Grab your Louis Vuitton steamer trunks (don't we wish!), and pack glam, 'cuz the glittery road is callin' . . . GO . . . GO . . . GIRL!

Everything sparkles in . . . Las Vegas, NV—The Vegas aesthetic drives me wild! The Pesky-ness is in visual abundance. It's as if Jayne Mansfield, Liberace, and Elvis all drank the growth potion from *Village of the Giants*, did tequila shots, then hurled in the middle of the desert to create their own city of sinful sparkle!

Old-school vacation place, rampant with hep '60s architecture . . . Palm Springs, CA—Features former homes of both Elvis and Frank Sinatra. This is where I go when I want to zone out by the pool, drink virgin banana daiquiris, and wear my Pucci bathing suit. **P**.esky **S**.ecret: Marilyn Monroe was "discovered" here by The Racquet Club pool.

The Pesky Meddling Empire will one day move to . . . Manhattan—What's not to love? Fifth Ave., Little Italy, Broadway, club kids chilling in Central Park on Sundays , the smell of roasting chestnuts wafting through Bergdorf's in winter, Liza Minnelli, and the best shopping evah . . . oh, je t'aime!

The Pesky-est, gaudiest & most glorious motel on the planet is . . . The Madonna Inn in San Luis Obispo, CA—They should just rename it Pesky Heaaquarters. Even the sugar is pink! The palatial psychedelic room I stayed in was called Dots and Daisies. Every room is themed . . . There's the famous Caveman Room, which is all leopard print and has a waterfall shower, the Old West room, tiki, pirate ship, there's even a circus room! Whenever I visit my sister in San Francisco, along the way I always stop at their coffee shop, which is called, amazingly enough, Let's Eat and Forever Be Happy! This is one of my fave places on earth, and an essential Pesky detour on any drive up the California coast.

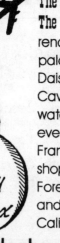

Travel Play and Relax

List all the places you've traveled: _____

_____ **Which Pesky place would you recommend I visit, and why?**

_____

_____

_____

★ Pesky tips for packing Your Wardrobe:

Instead of folding your clothes in your suitcase . . . roll them up like little burritos. I do this when I travel, so I can rock wrinkle-free.

Call your hotel before leaving your house to find out what the weather will be like when you arrive.

Remember: Sparkly accessories can turn almost any simple black day dress into an instant evening gown.

Bring a pair of jeans even if you're going to Marrakech in 100° weather. I always bring some, and I always wind up wearing them more than anything else I packed.

Take one thing that is warmer (a sweater) and one thing cooler (a slip dress) than you think you'll need for your destinations climate. It just may be the thing you end up wearing every day.

Instead of packing a full bottle of your fave perfume, go to the mall and get some tiny disposable samples of it.

Ziplocs make the best travel makeup bags. Sometimes air pressure during flights will make sealed bottles (like shampoo) explode in your suitcase! So, instead of ruining something nice . . . use disposable ziplocs!

Don't pack a stuffed suitcase. Knowing us shopaholics, we'll expand as we travel (and hopefully not in our bellies).

Trip Out!

Pesky Airlines

127

Jennifur's Guide to Glitzy, Glammy, Glittery . . .

HOLLYWOOD!

I'd so love it if you'd come and visit where I live . . . So here I've prepared my own tour of the essentially cinematic things that you, being a Pesky Meddling girl and all, would appreciate. I grew up in awe of these places, and I know you'll swoon at their glammy-ness too.

The Hollywood sign—Built in 1923 as an ad for a real estate development called Hollywoodland, until 1949 when they tore down the last four letters. It's our city's most glorious icon. (Go straight up Beachwood Dr. for a stunning view.)

The Silent Movie Theatre, 1942

The Silent Movie Theatre—The only remaining silent cinema in the U.S.! It's like my sanctuary. Here you can view prints of films you won't be able to see anywhere else in the world. They showcase stars such as Buster Keaton, Clara Bow, Charlie Chaplin, and there are even "Talkie Tuesdays"! The theater has recently been renovated in it's original deco style, and it is truly stunning. One request . . . Could you please pick me up on the way? (611N. Fairfax Ave.)

Take a drive through Laurel Canyon—From Mullholland Dr. to Sunset Blvd. This canyon was *the* place to live in the '60s . . . Jim Morrison did, so did Nico, Edie Sedgwick, Janis Joplin, Joni Mitchell, and Harry Houdini!

Visitors Guide →

Sunset Strip

Where the sun shines on the stars of the stage and screen.

Grauman's Chinese Theatre—It's existed since 1926, so you've gotta give it props for that much alone! Where else in the world can you practically hold hands with Jean Harlow, Ginger Rogers, or Liz Taylor? Well, here you can, and compare shoe sizes too! I'll sit through any cheesy flick just to sink into those red velvet seats, gaze up into its ornate Oriental chandelier, and try to envision which screen goddess had their gold-lamé-clad tush in the seat before moi. The whole thing is a magical cinematic experience in one of America's last great movie palaces. (**P.**esky **S.**ecret: Randolph's hands are the same size as Clark Gable's, and I wear the same size shoe as Marilyn Monroe!)

Let me show you

PHOTO BY UTE VILLE

MUSSO & FRANK'S—This is Hollywood's oldest and my most favorite restaurant. It hasn't been remodeled since 1937, so it feels all spooky and haunted . . . just how I like it! Musso's was all the rage in the roaring '20s when hipsters like F. Scott Fitzgerald, Mary Pickford, and Anita Loos hung here . . . and in the '40s its regulars included Rita Hayworth and Orson Welles. Last time I was there, all three Beastie Boys were chowing at the table next to me.

On Location 129

★ the **HOLLYWOOD** look

THE BEVERLY HILLS HOTEL—Also known as the Pink Palace (How Pesky!). Everybody who's anybody has stayed here . . . including Jackie Susann (author of *Valley of the Dolls*), Marilyn Monroe during the filming of *Let's Make Love,* and Liza Minnelli with her 2 cats. The kitschy Fountain Coffee Shop is where I have to go once a week for a mean chocolate malt.

TOUR A REAL MOTION PICTURE STUDIO!—My faves are: Universal (the E.T. ride is a must!), Warner Bros., and Paramount. See how movie magic is made right before your eyes! Just be sure to call & R.S.V.P. first.

 Pesky Things to Do in Hollyweird:

Go on a walking tour of the old movie palaces on Broadway in Downtown. You'll see The Orpheum, the Los Angeles, The Million Dollar, and about 10 more. It's a swirly-gig of breathtaking sights! Call the Los Angeles Conservancy for reservations.

 Carry a travel journal and write about your adventures as a "location scout."

The places I dream of visiting one day are: ★
Bali, Graceland, New Orleans, London, Hong Kong, Iceland

List all the places you dream of visiting?

_____

_____

_____

And until my next venture out of my room . . . Ciao!

..**STAY IN** *Hollywood*

My fave ride at Disneyland is the Haunted Mansion . . .
What's yours? _____

130

I Love You

Love and Sparkly
Pink tiaras
until next
time...
Jennifer

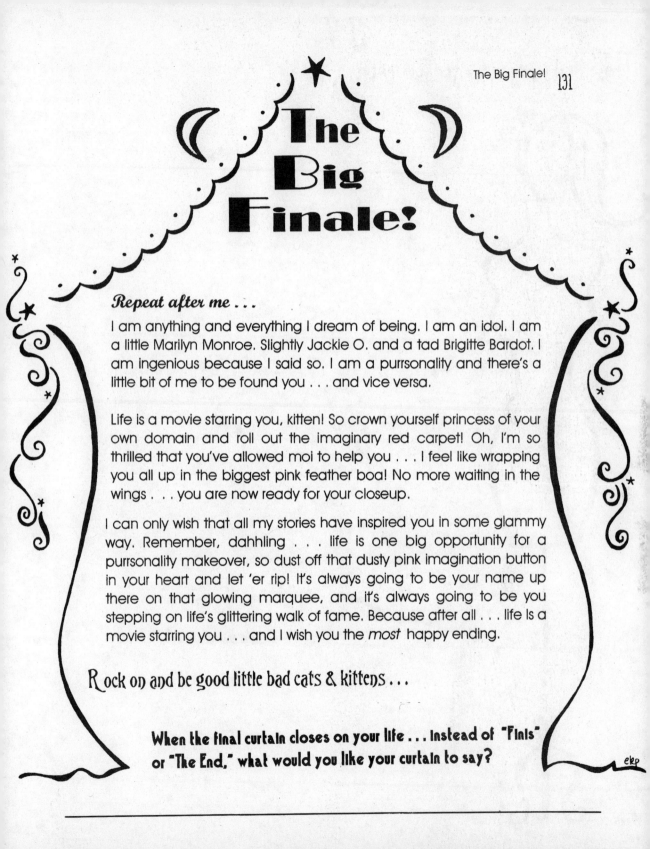

The Big Finale!

Repeat after me . . .

I am anything and everything I dream of being. I am an idol. I am a little Marilyn Monroe. Slightly Jackie O. and a tad Brigitte Bardot. I am ingenious because I said so. I am a purrsonality and there's a little bit of me to be found you . . . and vice versa.

Life is a movie starring you, kitten! So crown yourself princess of your own domain and roll out the imaginary red carpet! Oh, I'm so thrilled that you've allowed moi to help you . . . I feel like wrapping you all up in the biggest pink feather boa! No more waiting in the wings . . . you are now ready for your closeup.

I can only wish that all my stories have inspired you in some glammy way. Remember, dahhling . . . life is one big opportunity for a purrsonality makeover, so dust off that dusty pink imagination button in your heart and let 'er rip! It's always going to be your name up there on that glowing marquee, and it's always going to be you stepping on life's glittering walk of fame. Because after all . . . life is a movie starring you . . . and I wish you the *most* happy ending.

Rock on and be good little bad cats & kittens . . .

When the final curtain closes on your life . . . Instead of "Finis" or "The End," what would you like your curtain to say?

ekp

These Pesky pages are for your notes ♥

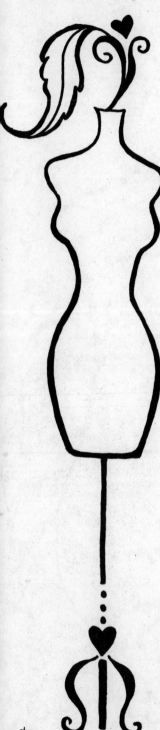

ekp